PURITAN PAPERBACKS

Gospel Ministry

John Owen

1616–1683

John Owen was born in 1616 in Stadhampton, Oxford-
shire and died in Ealing, West London, in 1683. During
his sixty-seven years he lived out a life full of spiritual
experience, literary accomplishment, and national
influence so beyond most of his peers that he continues
to merit the accolade of 'the greatest British theologian
of all time.' Despite his other achievements, Owen is
best famed for his writings. They are characterized by
profundity, thoroughness and, consequently, authority.
Although many of his works were called forth by the
particular needs of his own day, they all have a uniform
quality of timelessness.

John Owen

———————

Gospel Ministry

THE BANNER OF TRUTH TRUST

THE BANNER OF TRUTH TRUST

Head Office
3 Murrayfield Road
Edinburgh, EH12 6EL
UK

North America Office
610 Alexander Spring Road
Carlisle, PA 17015
USA

banneroftruth.org

The sermons in this volume have been selected from
The Works of John Owen, volume 9
This modernized edition © The Banner of Truth Trust 2023
First published 2023

ISBN
Print: 978 1 80040 329 1
Epub: 978 1 80040 330 7
Kindle: 978 1 80040 331 4

*

Typeset in 10/13 Minion Pro at
The Banner of Truth Trust, Edinburgh

Printed in Poland
by Arka, Cieszyn

Footnotes signed '—G' are from the William H. Goold edition
of 1850–53. New footnotes have also been added and the text
has been modernized.

The Trust wishes to express its gratitude to
Dr John Aaron for his assistance in
the production of this volume.

Contents

Publisher's Preface

JOHN OWEN pastored the Independent congregation at Leadenhall Street, London, from 1673 until his death in 1683. Many of the sermons preached during this period were taken down in short-hand by Sir John Hartopp, a member of the congregation, who then transcribed them fully in long-hand. After Owen's death a number of these sermons were published: some in 1721 and others in 1756. These were all eventually included in Volume 9 of William H. Goold's 1850–53 edition of Owen's Works.[1]

Of the forty-three sermons contained in these two tranches of posthumous sermons, the nine included in this book are connected in having the same theme. In each of them Owen takes up some aspect of the work of preaching the gospel – of Christian Ministry. The sermons were preached within a period of thirteen years and at a time when Owen had arrived at his final conclusions with respect to the nature of church government. Together therefore they provide a synopsis of Owen's most mature opinions on this crucial topic. Occasional footnotes provided by Goold point out where, in Owen's other works, a fuller discussion of the nature of Christian ministry may be found.

[1] John Owen, *Works*, Vol. 9 (London: Banner of Truth Trust, 1965).

Two sermons (1 and 2) on 'The Divine Power of the Gospel' (Rom. 1:16) emphasize 'the indispensable duty of everyone who wishes to be saved' not to be ashamed of the gospel of Christ. If this is the case for all Christians, how much more is it necessary for those who have committed themselves, or rather, have been called by God, to be heralds of the gospel and ambassadors for Christ?

The following three sermons (3, 4 and 5) were preached by Owen to Independent congregations at ordination services. These took place in 1673, 1678 and 1682 respectively. In 'The Ministry: The Gift of Christ' (Eph. 4:8) he explains how the gift of ministry is a fruit of the exaltation and mediation of Christ: 'There is a greater glory in giving a minister to a poor congregation than there is in the instalment and enthroning of all the popes, cardinals and metropolitans of the world, whatever their glory might be. Christ is seen in his theatre of glory as he communicates this office and these officers' (p. 24).

The necessary spiritual gifts and abilities required for ministry are communicated by the Holy Spirit. It is for this reason that gospel ministry is described as 'the ministry of the Spirit.' The comforts and encouragements of this truth are described in 'Ministerial Gifts: The Work of the Spirit' (1 Cor. 12:11). 'However much men pretend, therefore, that they are able to be ministers of the New Testament without these gifts – let them please themselves with whatever applause they may receive from people who are unacquainted with the mystery and glory of these things; let them despise and condemn whatever testifies to the contrary – yet, it is certain: where the gifts of the Spirit of God in the gospel ministries of the church are lost or neglected, Christ is lost and neglected also; the Spirit of God is lost also, together with all the benefits of the gospel' (p. 32).

In 'The Duty of a Pastor' (Jer. 3:15) Owen expounds the two essential tasks of a pastor; namely, to feed his church 'with knowledge and understanding,' and to pray continually for his church. 'It is in our prayers for our people that God will teach us what we should preach to them' (p. 37).

When a man is called and commissioned by Christ, gifted by the Holy Spirit, and ministers to the gathered saints, the church has 'access in one Spirit to the Father.' This is the essence of true gospel worship. The two sermons (6 and 7) on 'The Nature and Beauty of Gospel Worship' (Eph. 2:18) present an exhilarating description of the access provided for weak and sinful people with their weak and sinful praises by the mediatorial work of our great high priest. Owen emphasizes the wonderful truth that all gospel worship is 'performed in heaven.' 'What was the glory of Solomon's temple compared to the glory of the meanest star in heaven? How much less was it in comparison with the glorious presence of God in the highest heavens, where believers enter with all their worship, even where Christ sits at the right hand of God' (p. 60).

In the next sermon (8), 'The Beauty and Strength of Zion' (Psa. 48:12-14), Owen notes that pastors have a duty to investigate the ways and means of preserving and protecting the true Zion, the Church of God. He describes the 'towers, ramparts and citadels' that protect the church and will always preserve it. These are the King of the Church; the promises of God; his providence; presence; covenant. By observing how these have been at work in our days, we are to pass on our testimony to the next generation: 'For so many years we have professed the faith, we have walked in Zion, and found God faithful in his promise: not one word or tittle has failed of all that the Lord has spoken' (p. 69).

The last sermon in this selection (9), 'Christ's Pastoral Care' (Mic. 7:14), may not, at first glance, appear appropriate for a book on Christian ministry. It is part of the prophet's lamentation at 'the prospect of the sin of the people and the misery which was coming upon them.' Nevertheless Sinclair Ferguson's comment is valid: 'The Christian minister will find much help in [it].'[2] This is because, in times of declension, the ministry of godly men often has to echo that of so many of the Old Testament prophets. '*Our design,*' says Owen, 'is to increase the number of the godly, to convert men to God, and the result of this will be to preserve the nation. It will be discovered at last that those who are useful in this way do more for the preservation of their country than any army or navy can do' (p. 71). He shows that what maintains the prophet is his knowledge that even 'in the greatest flood of sin and judgment … there is still a basis for faith to plead with God for the preservation, safety and deliverance of his people' (p. 73).

It is worth noting that although the one theme addressed throughout is the nature, duties and consequences of true gospel ministry, none of these sermons was addressed to groups of conferring students or pastors but, rather, to church congregations. Apart from the ordination services they are examples of John Owen's regular Sunday preaching. This demonstrates Owen's judgment that all Christians

[2] Sinclair B. Ferguson, 'Some Thoughts on Reading the Works of John Owen,' in *Some Pastors and Teachers* (Edinburgh: Banner of Truth Trust, 2017), p. 302.

need to be aware of the nature of the work of the minister and to understand how Christ governs his church by those whom he calls to be his ambassadors. He therefore closes one of the sermons with the words: 'Allow me to speak one word to you who are members of the church: Know what it is that you have to do, with respect to those you have called and made officers today. Pray to God for a fresh communication of gifts to them. They are capable of receiving this. A renewed act of grace prepares and opens the soul for receiving new communications of God's grace in order to administer holy things to the congregation. Pray much for them to that purpose' (p. 33).

A companion volume to this work, entitled *Gospel Life*, is available. It is made up of ten sermons by John Owen on Christian experience, all of which are also taken from Volume 9 of his works and adapted into modernized English.

Sermon 1

The Divine Power of the Gospel[1]

For I am not ashamed of the gospel, for it is the power of God for salvation to everyone who believes, to the Jew first and also to the Greek.—Rom. 1:16

THE preceding verses of this chapter contain a statement by the author, a description of the apostolic authority by which the letter was written, and a gracious greeting to those for whom it was written. With this verse we enter upon the main subject matter of the epistle. It is, therefore, the centre-piece of this wonderful portion of Scripture: from it the first part of the epistle develops, and upon it the remaining arguments of the epistle depend.

The church at Rome had been planted some time before, but it is not known by whom. God, in his wisdom, foreseeing the abuses to which the facts surrounding the founda-tion of this church would be put, has hidden them from us completely. There is nothing in Scripture or in history to suggest by whom the faith was first preached there. It was probably by some believers of the Circumcision, from which arose all the disputes and arguments over the

[1] Preached on 19 May, 1670.—*G.*

observation of Jewish ceremonies which Paul had to discuss and pronounce upon in chapters 14 and 15. Hearing of their faith the apostle, anxious for all the churches and entrusted with 'the gospel to the uncircumcised' (Gal. 2:7, 8), writes this epistle to them to instruct them in the mystery of the gospel, and to confirm them in the faith and in the worship of God for which it calls.

In order to give weight to what he writes, and to commend it to their consideration, he tells them of his love and care for them. This arose from the responsibility which he had for them, in that he was 'under obligation both to Greeks and to barbarians, both to the wise and to the foolish.' He was therefore 'eager to preach the gospel' to those also who were at Rome (verses 14, 15). By these words he prevented any prejudice and jealousy that might arise in their minds, and answered any objections they might make to his writing. They might have said among themselves, 'What gives him, a stranger, living far away, any right to interfere in our concerns? Isn't he "over-extending himself" and "boasting in the labours of others"?' (things which, in another letter, he denied doing when responding to accusations of this nature). When his zeal propelled him to act for the gospel in some remarkable way, he was charged with these faults. To avoid this, he tells them, 'No, I am only doing what an honest man would do in discharging a duty which the Lord Jesus Christ has placed upon me because of my call to my office and my understanding of it. "I am under obligation both to Greeks and to barbarians, both to the wise and to the foolish." I am called to preach the gospel to every kind of person under heaven. My commission is to "go into all the world and proclaim the gospel to the whole creation" (Mark 16:15); that is (as explained in Matt. 28:19), to go to "all nations," as I have opportunity.'

Our Lord Jesus Christ, because of his love and care for those whom he redeemed with his own blood so that they might be saved, had given apostles to them – 'All things are yours, whether Paul or Apollos' – and he had charged these apostles to preach the gospel to them. When Paul, therefore, says 'I am innocent of the blood of all of you' (Acts 20:26, 27), how does he prove it? By adding, 'I did not shrink from declaring to you the whole counsel of God.' He frees himself from any idea that they might have that he was following some agenda of his own, or seeking some personal advantage by interfering in the concerns of the gospel, by telling them that he is discharging the terms of a debt. 'I am under obligation,' he says. It is wise for those who, in their differing spheres, have received the responsibility of preaching the gospel, to inform their hearers that, in absolute terms (however they might personally respond), they need not feel indebted to their ministers for the preaching of the word. It is our Lord Jesus Christ who has placed this obligation upon us. If we, in his name, pay and discharge this debt, we are sure of a reward; if not, he will require it at our hands. We owe the preaching of the gospel to those who are willing to hear it, and if in any way we withhold it from them we are defrauding them. 'I am under obligation,' says the apostle, and everyone who receives the gift and call from Christ is under obligation and should consider himself as such. 'I have done nothing,' says Paul, 'other than engaging in the discharge of the debt which I owe to men's souls.'

But another objection might arise. 'If he is so concerned about the proclamation of the gospel that he writes a letter to Rome – the greatest theatre upon earth, the head of the empire, the most famous place in the world – why doesn't he come here himself to preach it?' Paul answers this query also. 'That at present is not in my power. I am not my own. I am at the disposal of Christ's call and the Spirit's guidance. But "I am eager to preach the gospel to you also who are in Rome" (verse 15). I am ready to preach wherever God calls me.'

In case he has appeared to over-reach himself by speaking of going there to preach the gospel without having considered what that might cost him, he tells them in the words of the text the reason why he can declare himself ready to come to Rome, 'For I am not ashamed of the gospel, for it is the power of God for salvation to everyone who believes, to the Jew first and also to the Greek' (Rom. 1:16).

In these words there are:

Firstly: *A general statement providing the basis for what he had previously affirmed*, which is found in the words, 'I am not ashamed of the gospel of Christ.'

Secondly: *The reason for that statement*. 'I am not ashamed, because the gospel is the power of God.' This he then qualifies in three ways:

(a) With respect to its *purpose*: 'The power of God.' To what end? For this or that goal in this world? No. 'It is the power of God for salvation.'

(b) With respect to its *object*: 'The power of God for salvation.' The salvation of all? No. 'To everyone who believes.' To all believers: considered, either before they were made believers, or after they had received the word. To others, it is 'foolishness,' but to us who believe it is 'the power and the wisdom of God.'

(c) With respect to *the way in which it is administered*: 'To the Jew first and also to the Greek.' The word 'first' there refers to the order of its administration and not to any priority of efficacy or excellence. The word was to be preached first to the Jews, in many places, and for many purposes, of which you know and which does not have to be dealt with here. This is the meaning of the words of the text.

In order to expound the words, I shall consider two questions:

1. What is intended by the 'gospel'?

2. What does it mean to be 'ashamed of the gospel'?

As a result of these two considerations, the great reason for the apostle's statement, 'For it is the power of God for salvation,' will be evident.

Question 1. *What is intended by the 'gospel'?*

This must be answered in two ways. What the gospel is,

(i) *absolutely*: as it is in itself; and

(ii) *relatively*: with reference to our use and practice of it.

(i) *Absolutely, and in itself*: this also must be considered in two ways:

(a) Strictly speaking, according to the meaning of the word ('good news') it refers to the good tidings of the fulfilment of the promise by the sending of Jesus Christ. The name is taken from Isaiah 52:7, 'How beautiful upon the mountains are the feet of him who brings good news.' And in this sense, the apostle gives us a description of the gospel, 'And we bring you the good news that what God promised to the fathers, this he has fulfilled to us their children by raising Jesus' (Acts 13:32, 33). God sent Christ, according to the promise. It is this news that constitutes the gospel.

(b) In a larger sense, the word 'gospel' is taken to refer to all the things that were annexed to the fulfilment of the promise: the revelation of all the truths contained in it and all the institutions and ordinances of worship that accompanied it; that is, the whole doctrine and worship of the gospel.

The first meaning is what God does for us in giving Christ to us; the second is what God requires of us, in faith and obedience, and in the whole worship of the gospel. It is this second sense which is commonly meant by the word 'gospel.'

(ii) The gospel may be considered *relatively*, with respect to believers. What it indicates in this case is our profession of the gospel: everything that is involved in our fulfilment of all the duties of the gospel, when and as they are to be performed according to Christ's commands. I would wish you to remember this well, for I can assure you that your relationship with the gospel will be found to depend upon this fulfilment.

The apostle is referring to the gospel in both of these senses in this text: to the promise of Christ contained in it, to the doctrine of the gospel, the worship of God, in the first sense; and to its institutions, and every man's fulfilling of his own duty, according to the rules and commands of Christ in the gospel, in the second. These are the things which the apostle is saying he was 'not ashamed of.'

Question 2. *What does it mean to be 'ashamed of the gospel'?*

Shame, generally, is a grief, a disturbance, a troubling of the mind because of vile, foolish and evil things. These things make a man liable (so he thinks) to reproach and contempt and bring him to resolve to have no more to do with them, if once delivered from them. As the prophet Jeremiah said, 'A thief is shamed when caught' (Jer. 2:26). Such a person feels two things: fear, with respect to his punishment; shame, with respect to the vileness and reproach of his deeds. Shame particularly involves honour, esteem and reputation. Therefore, if you could remove the contempt men have for a particular action, they would no longer be ashamed of it. Men of the world have succeeded in removing from among themselves, within their own compass, the disgrace of sins that are among the most odious possible. Consequently, they stop being ashamed of them. We meet with men who are not ashamed of swearing, cursing, blaspheming, drunkenness, or even uncleanness. The wickedness of the world, within their own society, has removed any disgrace from such actions. But if they are caught lying or stealing, then they are filled with shame. It is not that the guilt and evil of the latter are more than that of the former, but that these are judged to be disreputable, and hence the shame that results.

We can think of this shame in two ways:

(i) Objectively, *relating to things which are shameful in themselves*, though men may have been strengthened against them so as not to feel shame. The apostle tells us that he was 'shamefully treated at Philippi' (1 Thess. 2:2); all kinds of shameful things were done to him. And all the apostles rejoiced 'that they were counted worthy to suffer dishonour for the name' (Acts 5:41). They suffered shame but 'they were not ashamed' (Heb. 11:16). It is said of apostate backsliders that they 'hold the Son of God up to contempt' (Heb. 6:6). The things which they did to him, in and of themselves, brought shame upon him; they deserted his worship and his ways as if he was not worthy to be followed. Paul is not saying that nothing of this kind of shame would befall him at Rome: that he would not have to endure any shameful treatment. He was led there bound in chains, he was thrown into prison. This is not the kind of shame to which he is referring here.

(ii) Secondly, there is *personal shame*. This also may be considered in two ways:

(a) As it affects only our feelings, as mentioned previously, when we may be troubled and confused in our minds because of anything dishonourable, vile or foolish with which we may have been concerned.

(b) As it produces consequences, when men, because of shame, have nothing more to do with those things which once had engaged them. This was true of David's soldiers, who had done nothing to be ashamed of, and had fought bravely in the battle against Absalom, but who, because of David's behaviour at that time, 'stole into the city that day

as people steal in who are ashamed when they flee in battle'
(2 Sam. 19:3). It may be that there is that light and conviction in the minds of most men with respect to the gospel
that it is something they would never be troubled or confused over, as though it was something shameful of itself,
and yet, at times, they may behave as men who are ashamed
when they flee in battle. This is the way in which the word
is used most often. As Christ says, 'Whoever is ashamed
of me … of him will I also be ashamed' (Mark 8:38). What
does this mean? What will the Lord do? He will not own
that man. This is what is meant by 'being ashamed of him.'

And this is what the apostle means here. 'For the
doctrine and worship of the gospel,' he says, 'and for my
work in preaching and disseminating it, I am not troubled
in my mind, nor will I desert it. "I am not ashamed of the
gospel of Christ."'

But you might say, 'Why make so much of this? I am
sure that there is no one here who doesn't believe that
they would be as ready as the apostle in such a situation.
Ashamed of the gospel of Christ! God forbid. What is there
about the gospel that the apostle here feels he has to insist
so strongly that he would not be ashamed of it?' To answer
this query, please consider three things:

Firstly, the apostle speaks here with particular reference to
his preaching of the gospel at Rome. 'I will come to Rome
also,' he says, 'for I am not ashamed of the gospel.' There
was at that time at Rome a collection of all the great, wise
and inquiring men of the world. What did they think of
the gospel? Paul tells us: a weak, foolish, contemptible thing
(1 Cor. 1:23). And of those who professed to believe it? 'The

scum of the world, the refuse of all things' (1 Cor. 4:13). There is gathered here the rulers of the greatest empire of the world – all the wise and learned men, the great philosophers, the princes of this world – all looking upon this gospel, its followers and its worship of God, as being the most foolish thing that ever engaged men's minds; fit for none but contemptible people. 'Yet,' says the apostle, 'in spite of all this, I am not ashamed of it.'

And we may notice here that there was not yet any actual persecution of the gospel at Rome, other than reproach and shame. The apostle is therefore declaring, by this word, that it is the duty of all men to stir up their spirits to confront all present difficulties, whatever they may be. The gospel is now loaded with shame: 'I am not ashamed.' It will come to blood: 'I will not fear to lose blood.' This is what he means by this expression of his present duty. For a man of his abilities and learning to face all the wise men of the world and be laughed at as a babbler, as one who only speaks folly, and still to say: 'I am not ashamed.' It could only have been the presence of God with him, together with a conviction of his duty, that enabled him to do it.

Secondly, for a sincere, gracious soul there is nothing in all sufferings more distressing than shame. This is why a large part of the humiliation of Christ was that 'he made himself nothing' (Phil. 2:7, 8; 'of no reputation,' KJV). He laid aside all the esteem that he might have received in the world as the Son of God. 'He hid not his face from disgrace' (Isa. 50:6). 'He despised the shame' (Heb. 12:2). To be dealt with as a vile person, as the scum of the earth, as the 'filth and dung of the city' (which is the meaning of the Greek word for 'scum' in 1 Cor. 4:13), to be carried past the faces of scorners, makes a deeper impression upon gracious, sincere spirits than anything else that can be imagined. It is a great thing therefore for the apostle to say, 'I am not ashamed of the gospel.'

Thirdly, there is also the figure of speech known as 'litotes' involved in the expression, in which, by denying something, its opposite is strongly affirmed. 'I am not ashamed'; that is, 'I am confident; it is something I glory in, I boast about. I am ready to do and suffer anything, according to God's will, for the gospel's sake. I am ready to undergo whatever God calls me to, or to fulfil anything he has appointed, for the gospel.'

The explanations of these two points justify the observation I will make from this text; namely:

Observation: *Not to be ashamed of the gospel of Christ but to own it, to assert it, to profess it, as something holy and honourable, in all the duties it requires, against all the reproaches and persecutions of the world, is the indispensable duty of everyone who wishes to be saved by the gospel.*

I shall not produce many Scripture testimonies to confirm this. But let us all be advised, in such a day as this, not to hide behind darkness, or to escape through ignorance of our duty. Consider what Christ has said with respect to such a day as this, wherever the gospel is professed.

I will give just one example, which is typical of all others: 'For whoever is ashamed of me and of my words, of him will the Son of Man be ashamed when he comes in his glory and the glory of the Father and of the holy angels' (Luke 9:26). The whole of the gospel is involved here: the person of Christ and the words of Christ. The person of Christ includes the whole work of the promise, and the words of Christ include all the commandments and institutions of Christ. We have already heard what it means to be ashamed of them. And what will be the end of those who are ashamed? The Son of Man will be ashamed of them when he comes in his own glory and in the Father's glory.

There cannot be any greater weight put upon words in order to strike awe and dread into men's minds. The Son of man, who loved us, redeemed us and gave his life for us, will come again (though presently he is absent, and we imagine that things are put off for a season). He will then examine our involvement in the gospel. At this time he will be resplendent in his own glory – the glory given to him as the reward for fulfilling the Father's will – and in the glory of the Father and the holy angels. We will be deeply troubled, then, to hear him say, 'I am ashamed of you.' We have the same statement repeated in Mark 8:38. The apostle gives the same great rule: 'For with the heart one believes and is justified' (Rom. 10:10). 'Being justified! Let us stop there. What more do we need to do?' Ah! but 'with the mouth one confesses and is saved.' In this confession is included all the duties required by the gospel, and salvation depends just as much on that as justification does upon faith. We cannot be justified without faith, nor can we be saved without confession.

You might say, 'How can this be?' To explain it to you, I will do three things. I will show you:

I. What it is in the gospel that we are in danger of being ashamed of, if we are not careful.

II. The way in which we are ashamed of it.

III. The reasons why we ought not to be ashamed of it.

I. *What is there in the gospel that we particularly should not be ashamed of?*

We should not be ashamed of anything connected with the gospel which is particularly exposed in the world to shame and contempt. The truth is that we live, or at least, have lived, in days where, far from being a shame to be counted a Christian, it has been a shame for a man to be thought of as not a Christian. It was not then the particular duty of believers to confess their faith in the gospel, because that was the common confession of all. The profession of the gospel in which many still trust these days is nothing but that conformity to the world which is cursed by Christ. In this sense, no one is ashamed of the gospel.

But there are some things which accompany the gospel which are, at all times, exposed to contempt and reproach, even when Christ and the gospel are generally professed. These are the things which we should make sure we are not ashamed of. I will give you four examples:

1. The particular truths of the gospel;

2. The particular worship of the gospel;

3. Those who profess the gospel;

4. The profession of the gospel that accords with godliness.

1. There are *some truths of the gospel that are held in particular contempt at all times*. Peter calls it 'the truth that you have' (2 Pet. 1:12; 'the present truth,' KJV). In the days of the early church this was twofold. The apostles had to deal with both Jews and Gentiles, and there were two specific truths that he particularly emphasized and would never omit. What drew contempt, reproach and persecution from the

Gentiles was that salvation should be by the cross (1 Cor. 1:23). 'It is folly to all the Gentiles,' says Paul, 'that salvation should be by the cross.' So what does the apostle do? Does he leave out this doctrine and preach others instead? No, he tells us that he 'decided to know nothing among you except Jesus Christ and him crucified' (1 Cor. 2:2). What was the difference when it came to the Jews? It was their insistence in adding Jewish ceremonies to the worship of God and to the conditions for justification. 'If I still preach circumcision,' asks Paul, 'why am I still being persecuted?' (Gal. 5:11). That is, 'If I preached circumcision, as they do, they would stop persecuting me.' Will he do it, therefore? No; he will not retreat; he will preach the cross of Christ and nothing else. He will preach against them and encourage all others to do the same (Gal. 6:12).

How then are we to know what are the persecuted truths of the gospel presently, so that we might not be ashamed of them?

In two ways:

(i) A man would have to shut his eyes very tightly, otherwise the whole world would show them to him. He would have to hide himself if he does not want to know which gospel truths presently meet with contempt and reproach in the world, for otherwise he would hear of them everywhere.

(ii) As a general rule consider the ways and means by which God reveals himself, and we shall find in those ways the truths that we are not to be ashamed of. Thus:

(a) God revealed himself principally in, and as, the person of the Father: the unity of the divine being acting in the authority and power of the Father in the creation of the world, in the giving of the law and in the promise of sending Christ. What was the opposition made by the world to that declaration of God? For the world never opposes the being of God, so much as the declaration that God makes of himself. When God revealed himself under the Old Testament, what was the world's opposition? Plainly, it was in the form of idolatry and polytheism. They wished to have many gods or to make their own gods, so that the true God became to them an unknown God. The testimony which the people of God then had to bear, and not be ashamed to do so, was to the unity of the being of God.

(b) But when the fullness of time had come God sent his Son, and he was immediately revealed in the love and work of the Son: the second person. Where now was the opposition of the world found? It lay directly and immediately against the person of Christ and against his cross. It would not believe that he was the Messiah, but called him 'a glutton, a drunkard, a friend of tax collectors and sinners' (Matt. 11:19). What then was the testimony required from believers at that period? It was to the truth with respect to the person of the Messiah, the Son of God incarnate, and to the work that he had to do. In that God was revealing and glorifying himself in the incarnation and mediation of the Son, the truths with respect to this Son were those which believers had specifically to speak of, and which the world particularly opposed.

(c) Where the gospel is now preached, the whole work of glorifying God is committed to the Holy Spirit. Christ promised to send the Spirit to glorify himself, to do the work of God in the world and to carry on all the concerns of the covenant. The Father laid the foundation of his own glory; the Son came, professing that he did not come to do his own will but the will of him who sent him, and promising to send the Spirit to do his will: to fulfil all the concerns of the covenant of grace. How did the world oppose God at that time? In opposition to the person, doctrine, graces, gifts and office of the Holy Spirit, as he takes Christ's place in furthering his kingdom in the world. And the great opposition that is made by the world against God today is directed against the work of the Holy Spirit in accomplishing the kingdom of Christ in the world.

Notice that the opposition made by the heathen in their idolatry against the Deity, against God, and that made by the Jews against the person of Christ, and that which is now made against the Holy Spirit, is all the same. The nature of the opposition has not changed, only its target. The opposition that was Cain's, and the testimony that was Abel's, are still the same. The one embraces the revelation of God; the other opposes it. The same principle that now acts against the Holy Spirit would act against God and set up idolatry in the world.

We may therefore see that God, in our days, has given a great and glorious testimony to the gifts and graces of the Spirit – as great as in any age since the apostolic period – and Satan has in consequence lost his advantage of denouncing the work of the Spirit by an open opposition of blasphemies and reproaches. Being impatient to retrieve that advantage again, Satan has raised up another spirit. One which would oppose the Holy Spirit, would compete with him and replicate his works. A spirit which, like the unclean spirit who threw into fire and water the one whom he possessed, now throws those whom he directs into all difficulties, so as to glorify itself. But whatever glory it might have gained by causing men to suffer and bear the rage of the world, there are three things that will reveal that it is not a spirit from God:

Firstly, the place from where it comes. It does not come from above. It is not hoped for, and prayed for, as the Spirit of Christ from heaven, who was promised. It is rather a mushroom that grows up in a night, the gourd of a night that springs up within them, and is called the light within them all. Now, the Spirit who does the work of God is promised from above, he is given by Christ and is expected and received from Christ.

Secondly, it is also known by its company. The Spirit who bears witness to Christ is always accompanied by the word. 'This is my covenant with them, says the Lord: "My Spirit that is upon you, and my words that I have put in your mouth, shall not depart out of your mouth," etc'. (Isa. 59:21). But the work of this spirit is to throw out the word of God from his church, to nullify and disable it. [2]

[2] Owen does not name this false spirit of his day and age. However, his description of it as being called 'the light within' and as devaluing the testimony of Scripture probably identifies it as Quakerism, which was gaining many followers at this time. 'By 1660, there was something like thirty or forty thousand Quakers in England, Wales, Scotland and Ireland.' Nick Needham, *2000 Years of Christ's Power*, Vol. 4, (Fearn, Ross-shire: Christian Focus: 2021), p. 265.

Thirdly, it is known by its work. The work of the Spirit of Christ is to glorify Christ. The work of this spirit is to glorify itself: to gather everything into itself, for judging, for ruling, for setting principles, and receiving all gifts.

This point had to be mentioned because I believe that the great opposition of the world these days against God's Spirit, his graces and gifts, and the worship he enables believers to offer, is found in this present false spirit. Therefore let us test the spirits, and not believe every spirit that arises.

This is the first thing that we are not to be ashamed of: the truths of God that are reproached in the world (especially those to do with his Spirit, his graces and gifts, and the revelation of the mystery of the gospel), and a pagan morality presented to us in their place. God forbid that we should be ashamed of the gospel in this respect: that we should fail to bear witness, as God is pleased to call us!

2. The *worship of the gospel, wherever it is found, is always exposed to reproach and contempt in the world.*

I pray that God will keep this always in our minds, that to be ashamed of these things is to be ashamed of the gospel. And we are guilty of this if we neglect to perform this duty commanded by the gospel. Men are ashamed of the worship of the gospel: (i) because of their shame of the worshippers; (ii) because of their shame of the worship itself.

(i) Ashamed of Christ's worshippers. These are usually the poor and despised of the world, for 'not many are wise, according to worldly standards, not many are powerful, not many of noble birth' (1 Cor. 1:26). Whatever work God is fulfilling through his people, they are viewed as the scum of the earth, as those who are to be despised by gallant minds and loftier spirits. I wonder what thoughts such high-minded people would have had of Christ himself, if they had seen him followed by a company of fishermen, women and children, shouting 'Hosanna'; and heard also the opinions of those Pharisees, that 'this crowd that does not know the law is accursed' (John 7:49). Isn't it true that men tend to be ashamed of the type of people that follow Christ? Should a man leave the society of the great, the wise and the educated, and join himself to these? Think of this, any of you who are, in any way, lifted up in society above your brothers. Don't be ashamed of them. These are to be your company, if you wish at last to come to glory. We must keep company with them here, if we wish to do so in heaven. Therefore, do not be ashamed of the worship of Christ because of his worshippers, though they might have no abilities other than that of loving Christ and worshipping him. Do not be ashamed of them because of the prejudice of wise and scholarly men against them, as was the case in Rome when Paul was not ashamed of the gospel of Christ.

(ii) Ashamed of the worship. The world is in love, and always was, with a gaudy, dramatic worship. They like to call it 'the beauty of holiness.' The Jews delighted in temple worship, the Samaritans in mountain worship. But the gospel called them both to worship God in spirit and in truth: to a worship that has no beauty except what is given it by the Spirit of Christ, and no order except what is given by the word. This is greatly despised by the world, and not only despised but persecuted. This has certainly been the case in the past. It is why the apostle gave that warning:

Do not neglect 'to meet together, as is the habit of some' (Heb. 10:25). The phrase 'to meet together' stands for the whole worship of God because the purpose of these meetings were for worship. Any who neglected the meetings, neglected the worship of Christ. Some of them did so when they were exposed to danger, and some do the same today. When a fair day comes, they attend the meetings, but when storms arise they absent themselves, like the Samaritans. What was the cause of their absences? The author explains: You were 'publicly exposed to reproach and affliction … you joyfully accepted the plundering of your property' (Heb. 10:33, 34). This made some withdraw, but you are not to be ashamed of meeting, nor of the worship of God.

This is the second thing that is exposed to the shame of the world, but of which we are particularly bound by our profession not to be ashamed of.

Sermon 2

The Divine Power of the Gospel (*cont.*)[1]

For I am not ashamed of the gospel, for it is the power of God
for salvation to everyone who believes, to the Jew first and
also to the Greek.—Rom. 1:16

3. WE are *not to be ashamed of those who profess the gospel*.
Our Lord Jesus Christ has laid it down as an everlasting rule
that in these he is honoured or dishonoured in the world.
And it is by this great rule that false professors – those who
pretend to believe in Christ – will be tried at the last day:
'As you did it to one of the least of these my brothers, you
did it to me … as you did not do it to one of the least of
these, you did not do it to me' (Matt. 25:40, 45). It is only
in these that Christ may be honoured or despised in this
world, for he is, in his own person, so positioned that our
goodness and honour cannot reach him, and the contempt
and despising of men does not concern him. This is why
Moses' faith is so highly commended, in that he refused all
the honours of the world and the reputation that he might
have gained and united himself with the poor, reproached,
despised persecuted people of Christ in the world (Heb.

---

[1] Preached on 26 May, 1670.—*G*.

11:23-26). He joined those who professed the faith rather than those of the world, with all its greatness – and this was his greatest honour. We note also the poignant prayer of the apostle Paul for Onesiphorus, when the later had discharged this duty: 'May the Lord grant mercy to the household of Onesiphorus, for he often refreshed me and was not ashamed of my chains, but when he arrived in Rome he searched for me earnestly and found me – may the Lord grant him to find mercy from the Lord on that Day!' (2 Tim. 1:16-18). Onesiphorus was a man of some honour and repute in the world; poor Paul was a prisoner bound in chains. He might easily have been ashamed of Paul but instead he searched him out and was not ashamed of his chains. To be ashamed of the poor professors of the gospel – poor in themselves or made poor by the power of their oppressors – is to be ashamed of the gospel of Christ, his truths, his worship and his people.

4. There is *one particular kind of profession that is, because of its nature, often exposed to the world's reproach.* The apostle Paul tells of it: 'All who desire to live a godly life in Christ Jesus will be persecuted' (2 Tim. 3:12). It is possible to profess Christ but not live a godly life, for there are branches that profess to be of the vine but do not bear fruit (John 15:2): men whose profession does not trouble the world and for which the world will not trouble them. These can so compromise themselves with the world and its ways that they do not have one drop of the spirit of Christ's witnesses, who trouble the men of the earth. But they 'who desire to live godly,' that is, to maintain a profession that will, at all times and in all circumstances, manifest its power, 'will be

persecuted.' We see many every day who are keeping up a profession, but it is not a profession that disturbs the world. This is to be ashamed of the gospel: to be ashamed of the power and glory of it; to be ashamed of the Author of it. No one can put Jesus Christ to greater shame than by professing the gospel without showing its power.

III.[2] *I shall now give the reasons why we should not be ashamed of the gospel of Christ in any way.*

I am speaking to those who are convinced that the gospel contains specific truths. If this were not the case, what would you be doing here today? I do not need to persuade any of you, therefore, that this or that worship, this or that order, is of the gospel. I will presume that we are all convinced of this and on this basis I offer the following reasons why we should not be ashamed of the gospel:

1. The first is this: because *Christ, the captain of our salvation, and the great example for our obedience, was not ashamed of all that he had to suffer for us.*

There are two things that aggravate shame and that weigh a person down with shame:

(i) The first is the dignity of the person who is being exposed. It is a greater thing for an honourable, wise, noble person of some reputation in the world to be exposed to indignities and reproaches and shame, than it is for beggars – poor, low persons of no reputation. Now consider the

---

[2] These two sermons were to contain three heads, according to the introduction [see p. 12 above]. The second head has either been omitted, or rather, judging from the nature of Owen's remarks, has been merged and included in the first.—*G.*

person of Christ: who he was, and what he was. He was the eternal Son of God, 'the first-born of creation,' and just as he was, in his divine nature, 'the exact imprint' of the Father, so in his whole person, as incarnate, he was the glory of all the works of God. When the apostle wished to emphasize the condescension of Christ in submitting to great shame, he noted the greatness and glory of his person, He 'made himself nothing, taking the form of a servant … becoming obedient to the point of death, even death on a cross' (Phil. 2:6-8). These three things, as I could show you, include everything that was shameful for Christ. But in that same place where he tells us what Christ did, how did Paul describe him? 'This took place,' he says, 'when he was "in the form of God, and did not count equality with God a thing to be grasped."' He was the great God in his own person and equal with the Father, and yet this honourable one submitted to everything shameful and reproachful in the world.

(ii) Secondly, shame is aggravated by its causes and circumstances. Various things cause shame. Some are brought to shame by reproaches, scandals, lies; some by poverty; some by imprisonment; some by death, made shameful by the manner and circumstances of it. By which of these was Christ's shame aggravated? By all of them, and inconceivably more than heart can comprehend or tongue express. He was reproached as a drunkard and a glutton; as a traitor and instigator of sedition; as a fanatic and beside himself. His poverty was such that, throughout his ministry, he had nowhere to lay his head, nor anything upon which to live except what good people gave to him of their own means. He was arrested while at prayer, when, as he told his arresters, they might have taken him at any time: 'When I was with you day after day in the temple, you did not lay hands on me.' He was taken by soldiers with swords and bludgeons as if he were a thief and a criminal: apprehended; carried away; hanged upon a tree (the most shameful death in the world at that time); surrounded by Jews and Gentiles to whom such a death was the most degrading. The Romans only crucified slaves, thieves and robbers: the worst male-factors; and for the Jews, it was the only form of death that was accursed: 'a hanged man is cursed by God' (Deut. 21:23). How did Christ behave as all these things came upon him? The prophets described his responses: 'I gave my back to those who strike, and my cheeks to those who pull out the beard; I hid not my face from disgrace and spitting. But the Lord God helps me; therefore I have not been disgraced' (Isa. 50:6, 7). Did he recoil, or withdraw from the work? Did he regret undertaking it? No; 'Your law is written in my heart, "I have come to do your will, O God."' Throughout it all, he 'endured the cross, despising the shame' (Heb. 12:2), until the way opened up for his glory.

This provides the basis for our argument: If the Lord Jesus Christ, the Son of God – engaged, purely out of his own love, in a work for us, poor, vile sinful worms of earth, whom he could justly have left to perish under God's wrath as we deserved – suffered all these things, never once drawing back or leaving us to ourselves, do we not have an obligation of love, gratitude and obedience? And not to be, in any way, ashamed of those few drops of this great storm that might possibly fall on us in this world, for the sake of our Lord Jesus Christ? Can we be disciples of Christ and yet think that in this respect we are above our Master? Can we be his servants and consider ourselves above our Lord? We are delicate and thin-skinned and wish all men to speak well of us, but we need to change our attitude if we intend to be disciples of Christ. What would be the result on the last day if he were to ask us what we had done with respect to our profession of the gospel? Whether we had observed all those duties which we had been convicted in our consciences we should fulfil: meeting together, to hear the word, to celebrate the ordinances, to pray, to fast, and all those other things required by the gospel? If we were to answer, 'Truly, Lord, we knew these things were right, but we thought that if we obeyed them we would have been exposed to all the mockery and contempt of the world. It would have brought trouble upon us and the plundering of our property. We would have been in great distress.' What else would the answer be, according to the rule of the gospel, other than: 'You must stand on your own. That was my day, and these were the things I required you to do. You were ashamed of me; I am now ashamed of you'? This, certainly, would be the sad result.

2. The second reason is this: that *whatever state or condition we may be brought to because of the gospel, the Lord Jesus Christ will not be ashamed of us in that state.*

I mentioned previously that shame is made up principally of dishonour and loss of reputation: being reproached for being involved in vile and contemptible things. Now if any man, whatever he may have been accused of, is supported in those actions by those who are great and honourable, he will lose this sense of shame. But this great and honourable person will not be ashamed of us in any condition: 'He is not ashamed to call them brothers' (Heb. 2:11). 'But what if they are poor and have been left with nothing in this world?' That does not matter. 'What if they are in prison?' Christ will stand by them and say, 'These are my brothers.' The original Greek word translated 'ashamed,' in this verse is used specifically with respect to the shameful things that may occur to us in this world. But notwithstanding all these, 'he is not ashamed to call us brothers.' Does he go even further? Yes: 'Therefore,' he says, speaking particularly of the present context, 'God is not ashamed to be called their God' (Heb. 11:16). What is the reason given for this? It is very clear. Consider the two parties that are in the world: the first, great, wise, glorious, powerful and at liberty; the other, poor, despised and condemned the world over. God comes into the world and sees these two parties. Which do you think he will own for himself? Would it not be a shame for the great and glorious God to own poor, despised condemned and persecuted ones? No, God is not ashamed to be called their God; their God in particular, their God in covenant, one who acknowledges them rather than the whole world with which they are in conflict. O that we could persuade our hearts in every duty that belongs to us, that Jesus Christ stands by and says, 'I am not ashamed of you!' God stands by and says, 'I am not ashamed of being known as your God!' Isn't this a great encouragement?

3. The third reason why we should not be ashamed of the gospel is because in *professing the gospel we are not called to do anything that is shameful in the judgment of any sober, wise, rational man.*

If the profession of the gospel called us to anything vile, dishonourable or unholy we would certainly have reason to be cautious in practising it. But is it any shame to acknowledge God to be our God, to own Jesus Christ as our Lord and Master, to acknowledge that we must yield obedience to the commands of Christ? Is there any shame in praying, in hearing the word of God, in preaching it according to his mind and will? Is there any shame in fasting, in godly conferring? Let all the world judge if there is anything shameful in these things: things which are good, useful and honourable to all mankind. The gospel does not require anything that is shameful. This why the heathens of old were wise enough, by the light of nature, not to oppress Christian meetings. Instead they accused them of carrying out shameful practices in their meetings. The view of the world was that they met together to pursue promiscuous lusts and treasons. This was their pretence because they did not dare prohibit their gatherings solely on the basis of what they professed. And it is still the same. Men do not realize that we will not, dare not, cannot take the name of God in vain, and prostitute the ordinances of God by giving the least suggestion of any seditious practice. Whatever persecution falls on the followers of Christ, they would rather die than misuse his worship by giving the least countenance of anything of this nature. The gospel does not call us to anything that involves reproach of any kind. If men would judge the strict profession of the gospel – praying, hearing the word, abstaining from sin – to be shameful things; if they consider it strange that we do not break out into the same excesses as themselves, should we be concerned with the judgment of such lovers of pleasure, who live lives of such continual self-contradiction? They profess that they honour Christ, but at the same time they reproach everything that is of Christ in the world. We have no reason therefore to be ashamed of the gospel: it does not require anything shameful at our hands; nothing that is evil or harmful to mankind; nothing except what is good, holy, beautiful, commendable and useful to human society. And we dare not prostitute the least part of any of God's ordinances in such a way that would encourage any disorder in this world, for by doing so we would be taking the Lord's name in vain.

4. The fourth reason is one which the apostle gives exactly for this purpose: '... *we are surrounded by so great a cloud of witnesses*' (Heb. 12:1).

In the previous chapter he had listed a catalogue of patriarchs and prophets of the Old Testament (time would have failed him to mention them all) who showed clearly that they were not ashamed of the gospel and its promise, whatever difficulties they suffered. 'And now,' says the apostle, 'you have a "cloud of witnesses": these great examples of holy souls, now at rest with God, enjoying the triumphs of Christ over all his enemies. Just like yourselves, they had to fight in this world against reproaches, adversaries and persecution and, by faith, they obtained this result: they gained the victory over all.' James tells us also, 'As an example of suffering and patience, brothers, take the prophets who spoke in the name of the Lord' (James 5:10). May the Lord help us to take the example they set us when they rejoiced 'that they were counted worthy to suffer dishonour for the name' (Acts 5:41). The Lord help us that we may not dishonour the gospel by giving any justification for the world to say that there is a generation of believers who have risen up today who cannot compare with those of the past in their profession of the gospel!

5. The last reason that I shall discuss is the one taken from the text, the reason given by the apostle why he was not ashamed of the gospel. 'I am not ashamed of the gospel,' he says, '*for it is the power of God for salvation to everyone who believes.*'

We talk of professing the gospel. 'What is it,' say some, 'other than pious talk amongst yourselves about unintelligible things?' This is how the world refers to the gospel. 'But,' says Paul, 'the gospel we profess is completely different to anything that you imagine. And we profess it, and will only ever profess it, as that which is the power of God to salvation.' If you show me that the gospel I profess, or any part of it, does not involve the power of God in it and upon it, bringing salvation, I will relinquish that profession.

But if you were to ask, 'In what sense is the gospel the power of God?' I would answer you in three ways.

(i) Negatively: there is no other power to be found in it.
The world saw that the gospel had great effect, but they did not know what produced that effect. They referred it to two things. Firstly, its content, which they said was only fictional stories, as we learn from the apostle Peter, when he answered them, 'We did not follow cleverly devised myths when we made known to you the power and coming of our Lord Jesus' (2 Pet. 1:16). Secondly, the eloquence and power of its preachers. 'It must be that its preachers are eloquent, excellent men that they are able to prevail so much over

the people and win them to the gospel.' No, says Paul. 'My speech and my message were not in plausible words of wisdom, but in demonstration of the Spirit and of power' (1 Cor. 2:4, 5). None should be mistaken; the effectiveness of the gospel is not due to either of these causes but to the divine power that accompanies it.

(ii) It declared the power of God; it made it known. This is what Paul says in the next words after the text: 'In it the righteousness of God is revealed.' It reveals to us the way in which God will save men. It declares that power that God will extend for the salvation of men.

(iii) It is the instrument of God's power. It is what God uses to fulfil his great and mighty works in the world. Preaching is thought of as a very foolish thing by the world. 'We preach Christ crucified, a stumbling block to Jews and folly to Gentiles' (1 Cor. 1:23). But God has chosen this foolish thing to confound the wise. And though its preachers are very weak men, just jars of clay, God has chosen this weak thing to bring to nothing things that are strong and mighty: the things of this world. It is therefore called 'the word of God's grace, which is able to build you up and to give you the inheritance among all those who are sanctified' (Acts 20:32). The plain preaching of it has this power on men's souls: to convince them, convert them, draw them home to God; to expose them to all kinds of troubles in this world; to make them let go of their reputations and livelihoods; to expose them even to death itself. It is the power of God to fulfil these purposes. God has made his instrument to that end. If it were the power of God to give peace and prosperity to a nation, or to heal the sick, nobody would need to be ashamed of it, but to be God's power for such a wonderful purpose as the eternal salvation of men's souls makes it so much more glorious.

The gospel we profess (all its parts and everything in which it engages) is that by which God puts forth his power to save our poor souls and the souls of those who believe. May the Lord never charge it to anyone's account that they have hindered the gospel in this purpose. It is sad if men keep corn from the poor, medicine from the sick, as they lie dying. But to keep the word of God from reaching the souls of men so that they might be saved, Lord, would you not charge this to any man's account!

The Author of the gospel was not ashamed of the work in which he was engaged on our behalf: he is not ashamed of us in any of our sufferings, or in any of the shameful things which we are obliged to undergo. The gospel does not require any shameful actions on our part; it does not place any responsibilities upon us which might justly expose us to shame. What it asks of us are good, useful deeds, honourable to all men. We have a cloud of witnesses about us, and if anyone requires an answer from us as to the nature of this gospel that we profess, we can answer, 'It is the power of God to salvation,' and this alone is the reason why we profess it.

I will mention further reasons to show why this duty is absolutely necessary, for, as I have said, we ought not only not be ashamed, but consider it an absolute duty not to be ashamed. It is necessary by *necessitate praecepti* (that is, by Christ's command), and also by *necessitate medii* (that is, by the order of things):

(a) It is necessary *by Christ's command* because he requires it of us. Therefore, on that basis, if we ever hope to be owned by him on the last day, we should own his gospel by professing it. All the world, all that is ours, and all the decrees of men, cannot free our souls or exempt them from the authority of Christ's commands. Let us look to ourselves: we are under his command, and no duty can be avoided if it is bound up with this rule.

(b) It is necessary also *from the order of things*. Christ has appointed it as a means for the great purpose of saving our souls. It is as possible for a man to enter a city without passing through its gate, as it is for possession of rest in Christ without professing the gospel and abiding by it. This is the way of entrance.

I have completed what I wished to present on this truth and from the many applications that could be made I shall only commend one to you. Without this application it would be utterly impossible for any of us, in the long run, to maintain a profession of the gospel. It is this: *Know the experience of the power of the gospel and its ordinances in, and upon, your own heart; otherwise everything you profess is a dead thing.* Unless you find the power of God active in your heart in the means of grace, do not expect your profession to continue. If the preaching of the word is not renewing your soul, illuminating your mind and endearing your heart towards God; if you do not find any power in it, you will soon find enough arguments not to risk any trouble or reproach for it.

But if you have experienced this power upon your heart, then the sense of being unable to live without it will rescue you from all relapsing, wandering thoughts. The same is true for all the means of grace: unless we can maintain an experience of their benefits and of the power and efficacy of God's grace in them, we can never expect to maintain our profession of them. To what would you bear testimony? To an empty, barren profession, that does not honour God nor does any good to your soul?

If, therefore, you wish to be established in this truth of not being ashamed of the gospel, remind yourself of all the blessings you have received from it. Have you profited from hearing the word? Has it at any time restored your soul when you were wandering? Has it comforted you when you were low? Has it drawn your heart to God? Remember the benefits and advantages you have obtained by it; then ask yourself, what has it done that you should now forsake it? And at every means of grace examine carefully what effect of God's power upon your heart has proceeded from that means. This will confirm and strengthen you, but without it all your profession is empty, having no significance.

Sermon 3

The Ministry: The Gift of Christ[1]

Therefore it says, 'When he ascended on high he led a host of captives, and he gave gifts to men.'—Eph. 4:8

THE purpose of these words is to show that the gift of the ministry and of ministers – the office, and the persons who fulfil that office – is an eminent fruit of the exaltation of Christ, and a great expression and pledge of his care and love for his church. This is the truth which I shall expound from these words.

Firstly, the ministry is a gift.

'He himself gave' (verse 11). The foundation of the ministry is the gift of Jesus Christ. You remember the question which he put to the Pharisees, 'The baptism of John, from where did it come? From heaven or from man?' (Matt. 21:25). Similarly, I would ask, 'The ministry: is it from heaven, or is it from men?' The answer is in the text, 'He gave': it is the gift of Christ. This was the great promise which he had made: 'I will give you shepherds after my own heart, who will feed you with knowledge and understanding' (Jer. 3:15).

---

[1] Preached at the ordination of a minister, 23 January, 1673.—*G*.

When would that be? 'When,' he said (in verse 14), 'I will take you, one from a city and two from a family, and I will bring you to Zion.' In other words, 'When I shall call you by the gospel, then I will give you pastors after my own heart.' That this is a promise of the gospel and is intended as such is confirmed in chapter 23, where the promise is repeated, 'I will set shepherds over them who will care for them … when I will raise up for David a righteous Branch, and he shall reign as king and deal wisely' (Jer. 23:4, 5). It was the great promise that, under the gospel, Christ would give ministers to his church.

It may be said, 'We know how Christ gave apostles when he was on earth: he called them, chose them and sent them. But by what means does he now continue to give ministers to his church?' In order that we might not claim an interest in a gift and a privilege to which we have no right, I will note four ways by which, through all the ages, Christ has continued to give ministers to his church. The church is to view these ways as the basis and foundation of the duties these ministers perform and of the work which we have undertaken this day.

First: he does it 'by the standing law, ordinance and institution of the gospel,' by which, as the great Mediator of it, he has appointed this office of the ministry in the church.

All the saints in the world, all the disciples of Christ (whatever necessity they might have seen for it, or however sensible it might have seemed by the light of nature) neither could, nor ought to, have appointed teachers or officers among themselves, nor would it have been blessed to them, had not Christ, by a standing ordinance and law, appointed such an office. If that law comes to an end, if its obligation ceases, the work of the ministry and its office must cease also. But if this ordinance should be 'as the ordinances of heaven' – of the sun, moon and stars that do not change – it shall never be altered in this world. It is clear therefore that to neglect the work and office of the ministry is to rebel against the authority of Christ. 'All authority,' he says, 'in heaven and on earth has been given to me (Matt. 28:18, 19). Go therefore, preach the gospel; behold, I am with you always, to the end of the age.' He is ascended, and he gives pastors and teachers until all the elect of God are brought to the unity of the faith and to mature manhood: to the measure of the stature of the fullness of Christ.

Second: The second thing he does is to give spiritual 'gifts to men,' by which they may be enabled to fulfil the office of ministry so as to build up the church in all its aspects. *Gifts do not make a minister, but the whole world cannot make a man without gifts into a minister of Christ.* If the Lord Jesus Christ should stop distributing spiritual gifts for the work of the ministry, he would not need to do anything more to terminate all ministry: it would come to an end of itself. Indeed, this is exactly how it does come to an end in apostasizing churches: Christ does not supply them further with the gifts of his Spirit, and all their outward forms and order, which they might continue, are of no significance in his sight.

Third: Christ continues to provide ministers by giving power to his church to call to that office men whom he has appointed and prepared by the gifts he has bestowed.

Three things may be noted of this power:

1. This power in the church is not tyrannical, lordly and absolute. It does not derive from any authority of the church but consists in an absolute compliance to Christ's command. It is purely the putting into effect of what he has commanded, and this gives virtue, efficacy and power to it. 'Do not look on us as though we, by our power and virtue, have made this man a minister this day,' says the church. 'It is in the name and authority of Jesus Christ alone, by which we act. It is in obedience to that which he has thus constituted and appointed.'

2. There is no power in any church to choose anyone whom Christ has not chosen beforehand; that is, no church can *formally* make a man a minister whom Christ has not made so *materially*, if I can put it in that way. If Christ has not pre-instructed him and pre-furnished him with gifts, it is not in the power of the church to choose or call him. And where these two things are present – where the law of Christ is the foundation and the gifts of Christ are the preparation – on that basis the church calls, and men are constituted elders and overseers of the flock by the Holy Spirit. It was the ordinary elders of the church of Ephesus who were charged by the apostle to 'pay careful attention ... to all the flock, of which the Holy Spirit has made you overseers' (Acts 20:28).

3. The way by which a church calls or constitutes a man to this office is by giving themselves up to him in the Lord, to which they testify by their solemn choice and election by suffrage. It is by submitting themselves to him in the Lord and witnessing to that by their solemn choice in his favour. 'And this, not as we expected, but they gave themselves first to the Lord and then by the will of God to us,' was how the

apostle described the saints of Macedonia (2 Cor. 8:5). This is the great work you have to do, today, in the calling of an officer; you have to give yourselves to him by the will of God, to be led, guided, instructed and directed; to have the work of the ministry fulfilled among you to your edification. And this submission in which the essence of the call consists (as I could show by many arguments) you must bear witness to by your suffrage or choice. When God ordered the Levites to be set apart to the service of the tabernacle in the name of, and on behalf of, the whole congregation, in order to show the importance he placed upon the consent and suffrage of the people, he caused them all to come together and lay their hands upon them: 'You shall bring the Levites before the tent of the meeting and assemble the whole congregation of the people of Israel' (that is, all the church). 'When you bring the Levites before the Lord, the people of Israel shall lay their hands on the Levites' (Num. 8:9, 10). In this way they expressed their agreement with the solemn dedication of the Levites to the Lord to minister in the tabernacle in their name and on their behalf.

In the New Testament the setting apart of ministers to their office is mentioned thirteen times. The first account is in Acts 1:15-26. It was while they were praying (after a sermon preached to them by Peter) that they went about their work, 'for everything … is made holy by the word of God and prayer' (1 Tim. 4:5). There was an apostle to be called. But in this case, God was to have a unique, sovereign contribution and to give a special indication of his own choice. It could not therefore be left absolutely to the choice of the church. But they went this far, in that, before God revealed his choice, 'they put forward two' (verse 23). This was the first action in the New Testament taken by a church, and it acted as the pattern for later ages. The church proceeded as far as possible, yet leaving the ultimate choice to God's sovereignty. 'They put forward two'; they acted to that extent, and then God took his man. But still, in order to preserve the freedom of the church in its action, even after God had chosen, there is the addition: 'he was numbered' (verse 26) – he was, by common suffrage, as the word signifies, reckoned among the apostles. They were beforehand allowed the choice of two, and, afterwards, allowed that he was of their number, by common suffrage.

The next appointment we have is 'the election of deacons' in Acts 6, where the whole matter is referred by the apostles to the body of the church. One wonders how such forgetfulness should have fallen on that world of men who call themselves Christians, to allow these matters to be done without the involvement of the church, as though the church were not concerned in them, when the whole body of the apostles (who had in their hands all the power and authority that Christ ever committed to the children of men) directed the church to use the power Christ had trusted to them. 'Brothers,' they said, 'pick out from among you' (verse 3). 'And what they said pleased the whole gathering, and they chose Stephen, a man full of faith,' together with the other six, who were all then set apart (verses 5, 6). Were all the apostles to be together now upon the earth, in the presence of a true church of Christ, called according to his mind, they would not dare to deprive the church of their freedom. But this is being done all the time now, as you know, by men who are far from being apostles.

It arises in another Scripture in Acts 14:23: 'And when they had appointed elders for them in every church, etc.' I confess that I am not able now to argue from this passage, although it is the most convincing, because it depends purely and solely upon the significance of the original word. But I would *suggest* to you that before *partiality* had guided men as to what was best for them to do, all the translations extant in English read this text as, 'when they had appointed elders by election.' This is what the word signifies, and this is what you will find in your old translations. It has been subsequently omitted to serve a purpose.

We may freely say, however, that there is not one instance to be found in the whole of the New Testament with respect to the method of appointing a person to an office, where it is not mentioned that it was done by an election carried out by the assembly or the whole body of the church.

This is the third way by which Christ continues to give these gifts to his church.

Fourth: The fourth way is, by his law, ordinance and institution, that the person, who is thus qualified and called, should be solemnly set apart 'by prayer and fasting,' as we have it in Acts 14:23. 'And when they had appointed elders for them (elected them elders) in every church, with prayers and fasting they committed them to the Lord.' On a similar occasion, when Paul and Barnabas were to be set apart again for a special work, it is mentioned: 'after fasting and praying … they sent them off' (Acts 13:3).

These then are the four ways by which to answer that great question: *How does Christ continue to give ministers to the church?* He does it by his law in constituting the office

– the law in the gospel, which is an everlasting ordinance; he does it by his Spirit, communicating gifts to the persons; he does it by the calling of them by the church, and by the church's submission to them according to God's will, and their witness to that submission by their choice of them; he does it by his ordinance of setting them apart solemnly with prayer and fasting. And these, brothers, are the matters for which we have come together today. This is our faith; this is our warrant. In this we are not following our own imaginations, or the inventions of men, or cleverly devised myths, but, from first to last, we have our warrant from Christ. May the good Lord pardon us if we come short in any part of our preparation of the sanctuary, and may he accept us according to the desire of our hearts to serve his house and his tabernacle.

I will only speak a word or two of *application* on this point, and then we will proceed to that which is your part of today's work. If God gives me strength, I will add some further relevant instruction, and then look to the help of the brethren present to carry it out.

Firstly then, if any office exists, however glorious or specious a title it has, which Christ has not appointed by virtue of gospel ordinance and institution, it is a nullity, it is invalid. It is no gift of Christ. Whoever holds and discharges it, by whatever formality they may have entered it – popes, cardinals, metropolitan bishops, diocesan bishops – that office is not valid, for there is no law, ordinance or institution of Christ appointing it. All the outward order and solemnity in the world and all the holiness of the person holding the office, cannot give it a right and title, because it does not have Christ's law as a foundation.

And where the office itself is appointed by Christ, but there has been no communication of gifts to the person, the office in and of itself is not a nullity, but there is an invalidity relating to the person. It is essential to the office that Christ chooses the person by communicating his gifts to him. Where this is not the case, I will not say that *every* appointment is invalid (because circumstances vary greatly), but there is certainly a disqualification in the person ministering before Christ.

Secondly, let the church consider properly how they are to receive the minister coming to them according to this law, order and institution of Christ that I have described, and the manner in which they are to view him. He is a gift from Christ. It requires wisdom and discretion in a man to receive a gift (think of what he is doing: he is putting himself under an obligation); much more is this the case if he is receiving a gift from a prince. But to receive a gift, and so great a gift, from Christ! There certainly should be some particular preparation of heart for that. How great a mercy it is, and how great a gift, I could easily demonstrate.

I will just name two things: (i) We must value him highly with thankfulness; (ii) we must progress under his ministry. As soon as we are a church of God, these things are expected of us. When we receive so great a gift from Christ, he expects that it should be valued, thankfully received, and duly improved.

And on the part of the person called, or of any one of us who has been called to the ministry, we are certainly required to behave ourselves and approve ourselves so as to lay claim to being a gift of Christ to the church, and be owned by the church as a gift of Christ. On my part, I do not know of a more fearful thought that a minister has, or can have, when thinking of the office, work and duty to which he is called, than this one: 'How shall I live so as to be considered as a gift from Christ given to the church?'

There are three things required from anyone who is to be accepted as a gift given by Christ to the church: (i) An *imitation of Christ*; (ii) A *representation of him*; (iii) *Zeal for him*.

(i) *An imitation of Christ*, as the great shepherd of the flock, in meekness, in care, in love, in tenderness towards the whole flock. This is how Christ is described: 'He will tend his flock like a shepherd; he will gather the lambs in his arms; he will carry them in his bosom, and gently lead those that are with young' (Isa. 40:11). Here is the great pattern; here is an example for all who are shepherds of the flock under Christ (who intend to give an acceptable account to the great shepherd of the sheep, when he appears on the last day). In meekness and humility they are to provide help and assistance, to bear with all things, and especially to conform to him who knows how to have compassion on the ignorant and on those who are out of the way.

(ii) *A representation of Christ* is required, with respect to all his offices:

(a) A representation of him in the rule and conduct of the church, so that the church, seeing our rule and conduct, may be sensible that the government of Christ is spiritual and holy. What a woeful representation of Christ is made by men who undertake to rule the church with rods and axes, with fire and faggot! This is to represent a devouring tyrant to the world, rather than the meek and holy King of the church. It is our great work, to whatever degree Christ has given us of the rule of the church, to represent him as spiritual, holy and meek: as tending in all situations to edification and not to destruction.

(b) A representation of Christ in his prophetic office. He was the great teacher of the church, and the principal work of ministers is to 'preach the word … in season and out of season'; to increase the knowledge of God, and of our Lord and Saviour Jesus Christ, in the church by all means. 'I will give you shepherds … who will feed you with knowledge and understanding' (Jer. 3:15). Any who take it upon themselves to be pastors, and who neglect this work of feeding the flock, might as well, with less work, and equal modesty, renounce Jesus Christ.

(c) Christ is to be represented in that aspect of his priestly office which may be imitated; that is, in continually praying and interceding for the church, and particularly for that church to which we belong. The apostle speaks of this: 'Epaphras, who is one of you' (that is, he was one of their elders and teachers), 'a servant of Christ Jesus, greets you, always struggling on your behalf in his prayers, that you may stand mature and fully assured in all the will of God' (Col. 4:12).

It is a great work to represent Christ in all these ways, in all his offices, to the church, and indeed, I might add: 'Who is sufficient for these things?'

(iii) *Zeal for Christ*. He who comes as an ambassador from Christ, in Christ's place, will have a zeal for all Christ's concerns in the church: for his worship, for the purity of his ordinances, for the conversion of souls, and for the building up of the saints. This is required from those who are Christ's gifts.

This is the first thing that the text teaches me: the ministry is the gift of God.

Having come so far, I will pause here and ask the church to attend to *their* work and duty. Afterwards, if God strengthens me, I will say something of the eminence of this gift, as it is set out in the text.

[Then the church approved the election by lifting up their hands; and the Doctor continued.]

I have showed you that the ministry and ministers are a gift that Christ himself gave to the church. I shall now show you the second element of the ministry.

Secondly: The ministry is a great and pre-eminent fruit of the exaltation and mediation of Christ.

First, it is seen to be so *by the great and glorious preparation that was made for it*. When did Christ give this gift? 'When,' says the apostle, 'he ascended on high he led a host of captives, and he gave gifts to men.' These words are taken from Psa. 68:17, 18: 'The chariots of God are twice ten thousand, thousands upon thousands; the Lord is among them; Sinai is now in the sanctuary. You ascended on high, leading a host of captives in your train and receiving gifts among men' ('for men,' KJV). You see that the words are spoken, in the first place, of God himself, and then applied by the apostle to Christ for the following reasons:

1. Because it was specifically the Son of God who appeared in this way to the fathers under the Old Testament. It was he who appeared to Abraham and gave him the promise, and to Moses in the bush; it was he who gave the law at Mount Sinai, and appeared to Joshua for the conquest of Canaan, at which time the church was to be set up. In each case it was the same person, though the circumstances were different.

2. Because whenever solemn actions were performed under the Old Testament, they represented, or were a means of introducing, things that were to be done under the New. How did God lead 'a host of captives in his train' on the glorious occasion of the giving of the law on Mount Sinai? That was the day when he set his people free. They had no rule, no order, no form of government before that day and had hardly shaken free of their circumstances under an Egyptian captivity. God had now conquered Pharaoh and triumphed gloriously over him in the Red Sea: over him and his host, who had kept his people under bondage for so long. He led captivity captive, and brought forth his people into liberty, though it was only the beginning of liberty. It was a bondage compared to what was to follow, but was truly a beginning of liberty for them. And all this was intended to represent the glorious conquest of the ascension of Christ, when 'he disarmed the rulers and authorities and put them to open shame, by triumphing over them in it,' or in himself (Col. 2:15). When he disarmed Pharaoh, he triumphed over him gloriously: 'The horse and his rider he has thrown into the sea.' In this action, the same divine person was fulfilling, typically, what

he would do pre-eminently when he disarmed rulers and authorities – Satan, death, hell, sin, and all the spiritual enemies of the church – triumphing over them. Truly, then, he led a host of captives. You therefore notice the change in the wording, which all commentators point out. In the Psalms it says, 'You ascended on high, leading a host of captives in your train and receiving gifts among men.' In my text, it reads, 'When he ascended on high he led a host of captives, and he gave gifts to men.' Though Christ is spoken of as God in Psalm 68, and as such was incapable of receiving gifts, yet in the mystery of prophetic vision he was described in that state and condition in which he might receive them, and do so in order to give them, as in Acts 2:32, 33. When he was exalted on the right hand of God and received the gift of the Spirit, he then gave it to men.

For what was all this preparation intended? What is it that is ushered in by the apostle upon this theatre of glory? It is nothing less than the giving of ministers to the church. 'He ascended on high, he led a host of captives, and he gave gifts to men.' What were these? Some were pastors and teachers. *There is a greater glory in giving a minister to a poor congregation than there is in the instalment and enthroning of all the popes, cardinals and metropolitans of the world, whatever their glory might be. Christ is seen in his theatre of glory as he communicates this office and these officers.*

What does this glory consist of, you might ask? You see no beauty, no majesty, in it, and nor did the unbelieving world in the person of Christ, or in Christ's ways. Wasn't there considerable glory in the setting apart of Aaron to his service, in all his glorious garments and ornaments, and with all the solemnity of sacrifices that were then offered?

Doubtless, there was. But the apostle says, 'What once had glory has come to have no glory at all, because of the glory' (of the ministry of the Spirit) 'that surpasses it' (2 Cor. 3:10). The reason why we do not see its glory is because we are carnal. It is a spiritual glory. God himself presides over today's work. 'I will make my dwelling among you … and I will walk among you and will be your God' (Lev. 26:11, 12). If we are the church and tabernacle of God, God walks among us this day. Christ is among us by his special presence. 'Where two or three are gathered in my name, there am I among them' (Matt. 18:20). And how much more may his presence be expected in the great transaction of his authority in which we are now engaged. The holy and elect angels are present with us, to give glory to the solemnity. We find the apostle charging Timothy, 'In the presence of God and of Christ Jesus and of the elect angels I charge you to keep these rules' (1 Tim. 5:21). Why the elect angels? Because they are present as *witnesses* of the appointing of authority from Christ. You have thousands more witnesses than you can see; there are more eyes upon you than you are aware of. God is present, Christ is present, the elect angels are present. These things are the true and faithful sayings of God. Here, then, is glory and beauty, in that it not only a gift but a pre-eminent gift.

Second, it is glorious and pre-eminent *from its foundation and source*, namely the humiliation and death of Christ. 'In saying, "He ascended," what does it mean but that he had also descended into the lower parts of the earth?' (Eph. 4:9). Why does the apostle mention Christ's descent here? Was it just to pick up on a word? Having mentioned his ascent, would he throw in a mention of his descent? No, that is not how the Holy Spirit proceeds. There was no absolute reason to mention it here; it must therefore have been introduced with reference to some particular truth. 'There is something,' he is saying, 'in Christ's descent into the lower parts of the earth that contributes to this great gift of the ministry.'

'The lower parts of the earth' could be interpreted in two ways. It may be referring: (a) to the whole earth, the world; or (b) to some parts of the earth in distinction to some other parts.

(a) If you take it in the first sense, Christ's descent into the lower parts of the earth (that is, into the lower parts of the creation, which the earth is), then it is the incarnation of Christ and his humiliation to which he is referring. This is expressed in John 3:13, 'No one has ascended into heaven except he who descended from heaven, the Son of Man, etc.' Christ descended and came down by taking our nature upon him. This may be what is meant here. 'He descended into the lower parts of the earth,' that is, 'He came and assumed our nature and was here in a state of humiliation.'

(b) Or, 'the lower parts of the earth' is distinguishing between different parts of the earth, that is, there is a reference here to *the grave*: 'He descended into the grave.' Christ's burial, which was a very great and clear testimony of the reality of his death, is what is being referred to. This is how I understand the verse. The apostle is speaking of the very descent of Christ into the grave, which is the lowest part of the earth into which mankind descends.

And notice from this that the death of Christ has great influence upon this gift of ministry. The gift is a branch that grew out of the grave of Christ. However lightly men esteem it, had not Christ died for it we would not have had a ministry in the world.

The ministry relates in two ways to Christ's death:

1. Because it was necessary in order for him to receive that power by which alone he is able to give ministers.
We find this in the passage Philippians 2:6-11. It was his humbling of himself to the point of death, even death on a cross, that was necessary in order that he know that exaltation by which he received power to give ministers. The mediatorial authority of Christ by which he was enabled to give ministers to the church was founded on his death.

2. It has respect to his death because the very purpose of the ministry is to preach that peace to mankind which was made by the death of Christ: 'He himself is our peace' (Eph. 2:14): he has made peace for us; and 'He came and preached peace to you who were far off and peace to those who were near' (verse 17). How did Christ come to preach peace to the Gentiles – to those who were far off? Specifically, by instituting the office of the ministry and sending his ministers to preach peace to them. And we who are ministers may realize the close relationship between our office and the death of Christ, which will strongly direct us in the work we have to do, namely, as I have said, to preach that peace which was made with God by Christ. This statement in verse 17 again emphasizes the beauty, glory and pre-eminence of gospel ministry: this great gift of Christ.

Sermon 4

Ministerial Gifts: The Work of the Spirit[1]

All these are empowered by one and the same Spirit, who apportions to each one individually as he wills.

—1 Cor. 12:11

You are a church of long standing and well acquainted with both the duty and practice of calling ministers. God has guided you to call men to officiate over you who have had long experience of the work of the ministry. I am sure, therefore, that neither you nor they have any need of my instruction as to our particular duties. I will therefore speak a word in general of that which is our station, work and duty, from these words in 1 Cor. 12:11: 'All these are empowered by one and the same Spirit, who apportions to each one individually as he wills.'

There is, on occasions, a disadvantage when preaching, especially for someone with my weak abilities, that either we must omit expounding the full meaning of a text, or else fail to emphasize what we wish particularly to draw from it. Both cannot be done. I shall therefore discuss only one main proposition from these words, namely:

[1] Preached at the ordination of a minister, 3 April, 1678.—*G.*

It is the work of the Holy Spirit, in all ages of the church, to communicate spiritual gifts and abilities to those who are called, according to his mind, to the ministry of the church, in order to equip them for all evangelical duties, to his glory and for the edification of the church.

Had I the time I would consider two things:

(1) Whether the Holy Spirit indeed continues to communicate *spiritual gifts*, as distinguished from *natural* endowments and acquired abilities, for the fulfilling of the work of the ministry; and,

(2) whether these spiritual gifts and abilities form the material call to the work of the ministry prior to any formal call by a church.

As far as the first is concerned, it is opposed by those who say that these spiritual gifts we talk of are nothing but men's natural and acquired abilities, with the ordinary blessing of God upon the ministry. There are no other spiritual gifts, they say.

And as for the second, it is denied that there is, or ought to be, any formal rule and order for calling men to the office of minister. They argue, furthermore, that any calling performed is good, valuable and lawful, regardless of whether the individuals concerned have these gifts of which we speak or not.

In these two subjects lie all the controversies about church order and worship that we have in the world.

But I shall speak only in general on the proposition set forward, namely that it is the work of the Holy Spirit, as he provides an able ministry of the New Testament for the use of the church to the end of the world, to communicate spiritual gifts and abilities to those who are called according to his mind. He does this in order to enable them to fulfil their duty in the administration of all ordinances, to the glory of Christ and the edification of the church. The proof of this one proposition, in which is the life of all gospel order, is all I shall attempt at this time. I shall do so by the following observations, principles and deductions:

First: *Our Lord Jesus Christ has faithfully promised that he will be present with his church 'to the end of the age'* (Matt. 28:20). It is his temple and dwelling place in which he lives and walks. This is the essential and fundamental difference between his church and every other assembly or society of men. Let men establish themselves by whatever order they please; let it be the order that they believe is prescribed in the Scriptures, or let them invent what they think is a better order; let them derive their right to power and authority from wherever they will; if Christ is not present with them, after they have done all, they are *not a gospel church.* They have no foundation. And where there is no foundation, the higher the building, or the more glorious its decoration, the sooner it will tumble down and come to nothing. I shall not repeat those promises of Christ's presence now, they are well-known to you. This is the great concern of any church: to ensure the promised presence of Christ with them. You have, I hope, under the direction of the Holy Spirit been guided in your choice of those persons who are able and faithful to go before you in the work of the Lord. But your goal has to be that in this way you may receive pledges of the presence of Christ with you, or else all other things will be of no value. There are some who care little for these things. Just build the house with such and such a frame; say certain words; believe that Christ dwells there – and there is your church, built and made! But the observing of all outward order and rules according to the gospel, will not constitute a church, unless Christ is received in it. Moses built a tabernacle according to God's mind, 'according to all that the Lord commanded him, so he did' (Exod. 40:16), but when he had framed it exactly, and set it up, and put everything in its place, it was just an ordinary tabernacle until the glory of God entered into it. It was the same with Solomon's temple: that was just an ordinary house until the glory of God entered into it. And suppose that we build our church societies according to the rule of the gospel just as Moses framed the tabernacle according to the pattern that was shown him on the mountain, they would still not be churches of Christ unless *the glory of Christ* entered into them. In this we have a difference and an advantage: the glory of God entered the tabernacle and temple of old in clouds and darkness, but the glory of God enters into the gospel church, under the New Testament, in light.

That is our first point: Christ has promised to be with his church to the end of the ages.

Second: *Christ is therefore present with his church, principally and fundamentally, by his Spirit*. There are three ways in which Christ may be present:

(a) He is present everywhere *essentially*: universally present by the immensity of his divine nature. Christ did not promise this because it is not something that can be promised. Promises are of *what may be*, not of *what cannot help being*. This presence of Christ is necessarily true, and cannot be otherwise, but it does not bring about an alteration. It does not make a church; it does not make one place heaven and another place hell. I am referring to the immense presence of the divine nature.

(b) Christ is, or may be, present *in his human nature*. This is what so troubled the disciples. He told them that he would never leave them, and that where there were only two or three of them assembled together in his name he would be among them. But later, he told them, 'It is to your advantage that I go away' (John 16:7). This troubled their hearts; they did not know how to reconcile these things. They were again told, later still, that he would go from them to such an extent that they should not look for him again until the day of judgment (Acts 3:21).

(c) There must, therefore, be some other presence of Christ apart from the essential presence of his divine nature, and apart from the presence of his human nature, otherwise how could the promise be fulfilled? 'I will tell you what that presence is,' says Christ. 'I will send you the Holy Spirit to supply the presence of my human nature.' This is the teaching of the fourteenth, fifteenth and sixteenth chapters of John. 'I will send you the Helper to remain with you, to enable you to fulfil all the work of the church. Therefore, though I am with you and have instructed you, yet you cannot fulfil any church work until the Holy Spirit comes. Wait at Jerusalem until you receive the promise of the Spirit.' After Christ's ascension, the apostles undertook no church work until they had the Spirit. Christ has no vicar, other than the Spirit. The truth is that the world grew weary of waiting for the Spirit, and took the work, for which he was promised, out of his hands. He, then, would have nothing to do with what they called 'the church.' I do not need to prove this. This has been the faith of the universal catholic church from its first foundation, that the promised presence of Christ with his church was *by his Spirit*. Some are beginning again to say in our days that Christ is only present in the outward ordinances of the church: his word and the sacraments. I grant that he is present in these, as pledges of his presence, and instruments with which, by his Spirit, he works effectually. But to make these the only presence of Christ with us is to leave us with a church whose standing is no better than that which the Jews of old had when in possession of the law.

Third: *This presence of the Spirit is promised and given to the church by an everlasting covenant* (Isa. 59:21). 'And as for me, this is my covenant with them,' says the Lord: 'My Spirit that is upon you, and my words that I have put in your mouth, shall not depart out of your mouth, or out of the mouth of your offspring, or out of the mouth of your children's offspring,' says the Lord, 'from this time forth and for evermore.' To whom was this promise made? It was made to the gospel church. See the previous verse: 'A Redeemer will come to Zion, to those in Jacob who turn from transgression,' declares the Lord. 'And as for me, this is my covenant with them …' With whom? With those in Zion to whom the Redeemer comes, to redeem them from iniquity. What is God's covenant with them? It is his word: *his word shall be in them*. If this promise were to end, and God were not to continue his word to anyone, wouldn't their standing as a church come to an end? This standing which is built upon the doctrine of the prophets and apostles, which is the word of God? Yes; take away the foundation and all must fall. God's covenant with a people is broken if he does not continue his word. And what about the 'Spirit of God'? He is also promised in the same covenant. Now, if the promise was not continued, then all covenant relationship between God and a people would be dissolved: for 'this is my covenant with them, etc.' says the Lord, as if he had said, 'If I maintain a covenant with a people, I will give them my Spirit to abide with them forever.' That covenant by which you are joined is dependent on this great promise, and if this is not continued, your standing as a church comes to an end, regardless of whatever outward order there may be among you. But he has given his church a covenant which shall remain 'for this time forth and for evermore.'

Fourth: *This is why the ministry of the gospel is 'the ministry of the Spirit'* (2 Cor. 3:6-8). 'Who has made us competent to be ministers of a new covenant, not of the letter but of the Spirit.' There were only ever two administrations, or two ministries, in the world that were acceptable to God. The one was 'the ministry of the letter and of death'; the other was, and is, 'the ministry of the Spirit and of life.' They were both glorious ministries. That of the letter and death was glorious in its *institution*. You know what glory belonged to it by its institution at Mount Sinai; by the way it was enacted in the glorious tabernacle and temple. It was glorious also in that which it *signified*. But 'the ministry of the Spirit [will] have even more glory.' There were ever only two ministries. If there is a ministry which is neither a ministry of the letter and death, nor a ministry of Spirit and life, it must be Antichrist's. The ministry of the law cannot be the same as the ministry of the Spirit because it is the ministry of the letter and of death, whereas the ministry of the gospel is the ministry of the Spirit.

Some people say, 'The ministry of the gospel is the ministry of the Spirit only because it is the Spirit of God who revealed all the dispensations of the gospel. Without him it would not have been within the ability of man's reason to have found them out.' In answer to this, we note that it was the Spirit of God who revealed all the ordinances and administrations of the law, from first to last, even the little additions that David made after Moses' time. 'All this he made clear to me in writing from the hand of the Lord' (1 Chron. 28:19); 'the pattern of all that he had by the Spirit' (1 Chron. 28:12, KJV). So that if the ministry of the gospel is the ministry of the Spirit, only because it was the Spirit that revealed it, then so also was the law a ministry of the Spirit, because the Spirit revealed that.

The phrase 'the ministry of the Spirit' must signify either that the Spirit is the *efficient enactor* of the ministry, or the *effect* of the ministry. If the first, then it is the Holy Spirit of God, by providing spiritual gifts and abilities to the ministers of the gospel, who enables them to administer all gospel ordinances to the glory of Christ and the edification of the church. If the second, the ministry of the Spirit signifies the communication of the Spirit, that is, he is the effect of the ministry: 'Did you receive the Spirit by the works of the law or by hearing with faith?' (Gal. 3:2), that is, 'Did you receive the Spirit by the law or by the gospel?' From which it follows that as long as there is the preaching of the gospel there will be the communication of the Spirit. Whichever way you take it, it is sufficient for my purpose. If you take the Spirit to be the efficient enactor of the ministry of the church, enabling the ministers to perform their work, or if you take him to be the effect of their ministry, either way, he is to abide with the church forever.

To clarify this, the hinge upon which all gospel order turns, we have therefore argued, up to this point: that Christ has promised the Spirit to be with the Church; that this does not consist of the essential presence of his divine nature or of his human nature in particular; that the Spirit is promised for the church by an everlasting and unchangeable covenant. The conclusion to be drawn is that the gospel is the ministry of the Spirit and life, and not of death.

Fifth: *Let us consider the reason why the Spirit was promised in this way to the church.* God has promised to Jesus Christ that he will have a kingdom and a church in this world while the sun and moon endure. 'May his name endure for ever, his fame continue as long as the sun!' (Psa. 72:17), that is, to the end of the world. It is said, 'Of the increase of his government,' that is, the church, 'there will be no end' (Isa. 9:7): he will order it for ever. 'On this rock I will build my church,' that is, upon himself, 'and the gates of hell shall not prevail against it' (Matt. 16:18). Christ requires that we should exercise faith in this promise, which we cannot do unless there is some basis for its infallible fulfilment. On what then does the unfailing fulfilment of this great promise which God has made to Jesus Christ depend, with regard to which we have presently as much reason as ever to exercise our faith? It must depend on some work of God, or of man. Suppose it depends *on some work of man*: that is, on the steadiness of the will of man in yielding obedience to Jesus Christ and thereby continuing his church and kingdom in the world. And also, suppose that God does not move mankind to this obedience by his effectual grace. In which case, God himself could only conjecture as to the result. Nor does this lay any foundation for us to exercise our faith, for the promise would depend on men doing their duty in the world. This, indeed, can be no real ground for faith, for what might prosper in one place may fail elsewhere, even under the same circumstances, and we know of situations where the gospel has been embraced, but has afterwards come to nothing. The fulfilment of this promise must, therefore, depend *on the work of God*. If you ask, 'What is the work of God upon which the certainty of this promise depends?' I answer, It is, alone, the work of sending the Holy Spirit.

There are two things to be considered in it: its *internal* form, and its *external* form. Its internal form is union to Jesus Christ by saving grace. Its external form and constitution is in accordance with the law of the gospel and its power, which cannot be continued without the continuing ministry of the Spirit of God with, and in, his church. To imagine the internal form (union with Christ, or saving grace) without the effective work of the Spirit is immediately to blot it out. If God should cease to communicate the Spirit by an internal saving work upon the hearts of the elect, the church would cease with respect to its internal form. No church would have any relationship to Christ as its mystical head, if God should cease to communicate the gifts of his Spirit.

And as for the outward administration and form of the church, whatever order you establish for it, it cannot be accounted a church unless the presence of Christ is in it. And 'no one can say "Jesus is Lord" except in the Holy Spirit' (1 Cor. 12:3). You cannot make any profession, administer any ordinances, or do anything that is acceptable to God without the Holy Spirit. The sum of all that you will do today is to acknowledge that Jesus Christ is your Lord: that you are subject to his authority, that you observe all his appointments, and that you submit your consciences to him who is 'your Lord and your God.' But you must have the Spirit of God and his presence in order to do this. The Holy Spirit is promised and given for the continuation and preservation of a church here below, and in this way to fulfil this promise which God has made to us, to continue with the church to all ages. And *if he should cease* with respect to either of these operations – his work of internal saving grace, or of imparting spiritual abilities for gospel ministry – *the church must cease*, both in its internal and external forms.

Having laid this foundation, I come, next, to:

Sixth: *A proof of this proposition, namely, that the promised Holy Spirit, sent and given in this way, furnishes the ministers of the gospel, according to his mind, with spiritual abilities in the discharging of their work*; and that, failing this, they are not able or qualified to do it; they are not accepted by Christ in what they do, nor able to provide a faithful account of what they undertake.

This is what the Lord Jesus Christ declares to us in Matthew 25:14-30. An account is given there of the continuation of the church, the kingdom of Christ, in the world to the end. The great Lord has gone away, intending to return again at the end of the world. In the meantime, he has appointed servants to take care of the administration of the affairs of his house and kingdom. To this end he has provided them with talents with which to trade. He gives them a different number each, as he sees fit; five to one, three to another, and one to a third; and he provides work to be done that will need all their talents. Some men have grown so rich in this world that they have no wish to use their stock, but this must not be the case with us. We shall have work to do for all our talents. No one has so little that he cannot trade. The man who had only one talent might have traded as well as he that had five, and been as warmly accepted. All commentators agree that it is spiritual abilities that Christ gives his servants with which to trade in the ministry of gospel ordinances. And the following three things are clearly taught in the parable:

(a) Wherever Christ calls and appoints a minister to the work of building his house, he gives him spiritual abilities to do that work by the Holy Spirit. He left no one at work in his house, when he went away, without giving him talents.

(b) For men who have not received any of these spiritual gifts to take upon themselves to serve Christ as officers in the work of his house is a great presumption, and dishonours Jesus Christ. It suggests that he had called them but not given them strength, as though he asked them to trade without any stock, or that he required spiritual duties from them but gave them no spiritual abilities. Christ will say to those at the last day, 'How did you get in here?' (Matt. 22:12).

(c) It is also clear in the parable that those who have received talents, or spiritual abilities, from the Holy Spirit must trade with them. And I do not know of a more necessary warning to those who are being called today than to charge them not to trade too much with their *natural* gifts, abilities and learning. These are talents of a kind, but it is the Spirit who must manage all the learning that they have, or it will prejudice them and yourselves also. *I have known some good men who have been so addicted to their studies that they have thought that the last day of the week was sufficient time to prepare for their ministry, though they employed all the other days of the week in other studies.* But your great business is to trade with your *spiritual* abilities.

Another testimony to this, among many others, is found in Romans 12:4-8: 'For as in one body we have many members, and the members do not all have the same function, so we, though many, are one body in Christ, and individually members one of another. Having gifts that differ according to the grace given to us, let us use them: if prophecy, in proportion to our faith; if service, in our serving; the one who teaches, in his teaching; the one who exhorts, in his exhortation, etc.' It is not my present concern whether this passage refers to offices or duties; but three things in the passage are clear:

(a) That it is referring to the ordinary state of the church in all ages. I confess that I would a thousand times more prefer to be of the opinion of those who say that the validity of all churches has come to an end – bad as that is – than of the opinion of those who say that a church may be a true church without possessing these gifts and graces. If I did not see these graces being continually given to men, in order to keep up the ordinances of the church to some degree, I would believe that it had ceased.

(b) That gifts are the foundation of all church work, whether it is in office or out of office. 'Having gifts ... let us use them,' says the apostle. If there are no spiritual gifts, there is no spiritual work. Spiritual gifts are the foundation of office, which is the foundation of work in the church and of all gospel ministries particularly, according to the gifts received. You may indeed think that it is wasted labour to prove this, but there is nothing that is more despised or reproached in the world than this belief, that there are spiritual gifts given to men to enable them to fulfil gospel ministries.

(c) That not only the discharge of duties and work depends on the ministry of gifts, but the measure of the work depends on the measure of the gifts. It is according to the measure that each one has received, and there are many different measures. As long as there is some measure of spiritual gifts, let it not be despised among you. The gifts of the Holy Spirit are not only for work, but also, let me stress, for the measure of work (Eph. 4:8-13). All these spiritual gifts the Holy Spirit bestows to enable men to fulfil the work.

Seventh: *In that spiritual gifts are bestowed for this purpose, it follows that they are necessary for it.* There can be no gospel ministry without spiritual gifts: the ministry of the gospel being the ministry of the Spirit, and all gospel minis-try being spiritual. The truth is that one reason why the ministry is called, and is, spiritual, is because it is not to be ministered to the glory of Christ except by the help of these spiritual gifts. If the Lord Jesus Christ had appointed carnal ordinances, suited to human strength and reason, there would have been no need for him to promise the assistance of the Spirit. The spirit of a man knows the things of a man (1 Cor. 2:11, KJV). Man's spirit will find out everything within the compass of a man, and give strength for their fulfilment. But Christ says, '"The words that I have spoken to you are spirit and life" (John 6:63), and all my offices and ordinances are spiritual.' Therefore, spiritual gifts are necessary for their administration, and hence, *spiritual gifts and spiritual ministries live and die together*. The way in which the world lost the spiritual ministry of the gospel was by the neglect and contempt of spiritual gifts, by which alone they can be fulfilled. This was the basis of the apostasy of the primitive church – they grew weary of spiritual ministrations. It is the most difficult and exhausting ministry. As men's hearts become more carnal they grew tired of spiritual things. They were not willing to wait upon Christ for supplies of grace and for the gifts of the Spirit. For these gifts are not grace, and they will not flourish long in a soil where there is no grace. Just as we would not produce so much sin were it not for our original corruption, from which it grows, so fruitful gifts will not grow for long except *in the soil of the Spirit*. How many people with gifts have flourished for a while, and then have withered because they were not planted in a good soil! It is great drudgery for any man to maintain spiritual gifts when these have no spiritual soil in which to grow.

The world grew weary of gospel ministry and would not continue in that way. Where did they turn? They invented new ways that suited their inclinations: they produced prayer-books to read, ceremonies to perform, and a number of inventions to maintain a form of worship without the spiritual gifts. We have an example in the church of Rome. What various extravagant things they have done in order to maintain an outward show, when they had lost spiritual gifts. All forms of worship do nothing except maintain an outward appearance. They did not like to retain these gifts in their minds, by which alone spiritual worship is to be ministered. The principle of the apostasy of all the churches in the world derives from a weariness of serving God by the help and assistance of the Spirit.

Eighth: *We argue from our experience that there is a commu-nication of spiritual gifts in all gospel ordinances.* We know how this is laughed at by profane scoffers, but we plead the experience of those who are humble and holy, and have a spiritual acquaintance of these things. I hope that I may argue against the world on the basis of the experience of this congregation. Haven't you had experience of this ministry? Haven't you found in the ministries of those whom God has called to lead you, evidences of the presence of Christ by his Spirit communicating gifts to them, enabling them to edify and comfort you effectively? Haven't you had proof of the Spirit of God speaking in them (2 Cor. 13:3)?

It is a shocking presumption for men to think of contin-uing gospel ministries without the supplies of the Spirit; as you who are God's people can testify. Every congregation of Christ can bear witness that the Spirit 'apportions to each one individually as he wills': he gives his assistance as he pleases. However much men pretend, therefore, that they are able to be ministers of the New Testament without these gifts – let them please themselves with whatever applause they may receive from people who are unacquainted with the mystery and glory of these things; let them despise and condemn whatever testifies to the contrary – yet, it is certain: where the gifts of the Spirit of God in the gospel ministries of the church are lost or neglected, Christ is lost and neglected also; the Spirit of God is lost also, together with all the benefits of the gospel.

Exhortation to ministers

I have one more word to say to those whom Christ has called to the work of the ministry, and whom you have called today, and that is *a word of exhortation*. I said at the beginning that I could not give them *instruction* but I may give them a word of *exhortation*, namely, to attend to the ministry to which God has called them on the basis of this foundation. And there are three motives which I can provide for them.

First: *It is the most difficult ministry that any man can be called to*; as it is so great, to that extent it is so difficult. Any other way of ministry is easy in comparison to the way of spiritual gifts: easy to flesh and blood. What an easy ministry, with all their altars and services, has the church of Rome provided for their ministers! To read, and to sing, come as they will, prepared or not prepared, having hearts and minds filled with whatever they will; here is a ministry for them that is easier than any trade, and in it they make use of their natural abilities and gifts. But if we define our ministry according to gifts received from the

Holy Spirit then the matter and root in which alone these gifts grow must be carefully preserved. If grace decays in our hearts a ministry in gifts will become a burden. It will be unpleasant to ourselves as well as being useless to the congregation. We must carefully guard the soil, or it will be of no advantage that this ministry has been committed to us. It is commanded that all ministers should be useful. Hand and heart must always be filled with work: 'Practise these things' (1 Tim. 4:15; 'meditate on these things,' KJV). If you have undertaken the work of ministry you must always be meditating on it. Unless you are practising these things continually you will not be faithful dispensers of the word. A man may preach a very good sermon who is not such a good man himself, but someone whose heart and mind is not always in the work will never make *a good minister of Jesus Christ*. Spiritual gifts will require continual thought on the matters of the gospel, and this makes it a difficult ministry. Our hearts and minds must always be cast into the mould and form of those things which we are to deliver to others. It is surprising how a little necessary diversion will so easily incapacitate the mind for this work.

Second: Just as it is a most difficult work to maintain success-fully, to the same extent it is a glorious work, however much the world derides it. The great purpose of the apostle was to show that it is so much more glorious than the old admin-istration (2 Cor. 3). The latter was a very glorious ministry, but that which has been committed to us is more glorious in that it is 'the ministry of the Spirit' by which souls are converted by the power of grace, and holy converse with God is maintained. To be under the eye of the Holy God, the judge of these ministerial gifts, is much more glorious than beholding the high priest in Solomon's temple. Therefore, do not be distracted from them in any way.

Third: *This is the only ministry that is truly effective in edifying and building up the church* (Eph. 4:8-16). This is the great purpose for which gospel ministers are appointed, 'until we all attain … to the measure of the stature of the fullness of Christ.' May God prosper it in your hands.

Exhortation to church members

Allow me to speak one word to you who are *members of the church*: Know what it is that you have to do, with respect to those you have called and made officers today. Pray to God for a fresh communication of gifts to them. They are capable of receiving this. It is a renewed act of grace which prepares and opens the soul for receiving new communications of God's grace in order to administer holy things to the congregation. Pray much for them to that purpose.

Sermon 5

The Duty of a Pastor[1]

And I will give you shepherds after my own heart, who will
feed you with knowledge and understanding.—Jer. 3:15

ALL the names of the officers of the church under the New
Testament have two senses: a *general* and wider sense, and
a *specific* sense. The name 'deacon,' for example, has the
general sense of a minister or servant; and it has a specific
sense in which it denotes that *specific office* which was instituted in the church to take care of the poor. In the same
way, the name 'pastor' has both a general and specific sense.
In general, it signifies any teacher or officer in the church,
ordinary or extraordinary. Specifically, it signifies that
particular officer in the church who is distinguished from
a teacher: 'He gave ... the pastors and teachers' (Eph. 4:11).
There is a distinction between pastor and teacher, *not as to
degree, but as to order*. I do not understand this distinction
in the sense of those who make bishops and presbyters
differ in degree, but not in order; it is rather a distinction

---

[1] Preached on 8 September, 1682 (*G.*), at the ordination of his
successor, David Clarkson, at Leadenhall Street Church, London.
See Crawford Gribben, *John Owen and English Puritanism:*
Experiences of Defeat (Oxford: OUP, 2016), pp. 259-60.

according to that beautiful order which Christ has instituted in his church. Christ has instituted a beautiful order
in his church, if it were only discovered and built upon. I
sometimes long that I might live to see it, but I do not think
that I shall. Yet, I would suggest to my brothers that the way
to discover it is by the harmony that exists between gifts,
office, and edification. The origin of all church order and
rule is in gifts; the exercise of those gifts is by office; the
purpose of all those gifts and offices is edification.

I believe that I can demonstrate that all the ordinary
spiritual gifts that Christ has given to his church may be
reduced to four categories. All of these categories are for
the exercising of the gifts, and each gift must be exercised
distinctly. This alone is the way by which you will find out
Christ's beautiful order in the church. The first category
of gifts is to be exercised by the *pastor*; the second by the
teacher; a third by the *ruler*; the last by the *deacon*. All these
gifts, exercised by all these officers, meet all the needs for the
edification of the church. The belief that the rule and conduct
of Christ's church is met by one man, or by all men, is a
worthless opinion. I am not saying anything other than what
is found in Romans 12:6-8. If we were to study that harmony
more we would find more of the beauty and glory of it.

In speaking of those pastors mentioned here in the text, I
will refer to them in general, that is, with reference to all the
teaching offices of the church: this is the general sense of
the word. And all that I have to say is to remind myself, my
brothers and yourselves, of something of the duty of such a
pastor: what is required of him; what is expected from him.
I do not intend to cover all the necessary duties of a pastor
or teacher, but only to give examples.

First: The duty of such a church officer[2] – pastor, teacher, elder of the church – is that which is found in the text, *'to feed [the church] with knowledge and understanding.'* This feeding is by the preaching of the gospel. A man who does not feed his flock is not a pastor. This work belongs essentially to the office; it is not merely a duty to be performed now and then, as circumstances arise (as is the view of the ministry held by the world – a dead idol). The apostle says it is: to 'devote ourselves to prayer and to the ministry of the word' (Acts 6:4). It is to 'labour in preaching and teaching' (1 Tim. 5:17): to make all things subservient to this work of preaching and instructing the church. It is to be done in that attitude mentioned by the apostle in Colossians 1:28, where he speaks of his preaching and the purpose of his preaching: 'Him we proclaim, warning everyone and teaching everyone with all wisdom, that we may present everyone mature in Christ.' How did he do it? 'For this I toil, struggling with all his energy that he powerfully works within me' (verse 29). Not a word in our translation conveys fully the emphasis of the original words. 'For this I toil': the meaning of which is to labour with diligence and purpose, with weariness and industry. I labour *usque ad fatigationem* – 'to the spending of myself.' 'Struggling': striving as a man who runs a race, or striving as a man who wrestles for victory, as athletes do in their public contests. And how? – 'according to the effectual in-working, or inward operation, of him who effectually works in me.' There is no word in

---

[2] Note that many of the topics raised in this sermon are discussed further in 'The True Nature of a Gospel Church,' *Works,* Vol. 16, pp. 74-96 (Goold), and also in 'A Discourse of Spiritual Gifts,' *Works,* Vol. 4, pp. 486-520.

English that conveys the emphasis of the original Greek here. And how is all this done? – 'with mighty power.' This is how the apostle approaches the work (it should fill us with dread as we consider it): 'I labour diligently, I strive as in a race, I wrestle for victory; by the mighty in-working power of Christ working in me; and that with great and exceeding power.'

What I intend to do is to show you, by using examples, what is required in this work of teaching or feeding the congregation with knowledge and understanding, as it is carried out by the duty of preaching the word.

1. The first requirement is *spiritual wisdom* in understanding the mysteries of the gospel, so that we might be able to declare the whole counsel of God and the riches and treasures of the grace of Christ, to the souls of men. See Acts 20:27; 1 Cor. 2:1-4; Eph. 3:7-9. Many in God's church in the days of the apostles were growing and thriving; they had a great insight into spiritual things and into the mysteries of the gospel. The apostle prayed that they might all have it, 'That the God of our Lord Jesus Christ, the Father of glory, may give you a spirit of wisdom and of revelation in the knowledge of him, having the eyes of your hearts enlightened, that you may know what is the hope to which he has called you, what are the riches of his glorious inheritance in the saints' (Eph. 1:17, 18).

It is truly not an easy thing for ministers to instruct to such a level of duty. If they do not possess a degree of eminence, how can we lead such people as these to perfection? We must labour to have a thorough knowledge of these mysteries or we will be useless to a great part of the church. The work requires spiritual wisdom and under-standing in the mysteries of the gospel.

2. *Authority* is required. What is authority in a preaching ministry? It is a consequence of unction and not of office. The scribes had an outward call to teach in the church, but they had no unction, no anointing, that would witness to the fact that they had the Holy Spirit in his gifts and graces. Christ had no outward call, but he had an unction: he had a full unction of the Holy Spirit in his gifts and graces, for the preaching of the gospel. A controversy arose on this point. The scribes said to him, 'By what authority are you doing these things, or who gave you this authority to do them?' (Mark 11:28). The Holy Spirit decided the matter: 'He was teaching them as one who had authority, and not as their scribes' (Matt. 7:29). They had the authority of office, but not of unction; Christ had only that of unction. And preaching in demonstration of the Spirit, about which men quarrel so much, is nothing less than the evidence of unction when preaching, discovered in the communication to the preacher of gifts and graces for the fulfilment of his office. It is completely in vain, therefore, for men to pretend to authority. To the degree in which they have evidence of unction from God in gifts and graces, that, and no more, is the degree of authority in preaching which they have. Let everyone, therefore, keep within his own bounds.

3. Another thing required is the *experience* of the power of the things we preach to others. It is surely the case that no man preaches a sermon effectively to others who has not first preached it to his own heart. He who does not feed on, and digest, and grow by what he has prepared for the people, may be giving them poison as far as he knows; for

unless he feels the power of it in his own heart he cannot have any confidence that it will have power in the hearts of others. It is an easier thing to prepare our heads to preach than to prepare our hearts to preach. To prepare our heads to preach is just to fill our minds and memories with some ideas of the truth, of our own or other men's, and declare them clearly enough to give satisfaction to ourselves and others: this is very easy. But to bring our hearts to preach is to be transformed into the power of these truths; or to find the power of them, both before, in preparing our hearts and minds, and in the delivery of them, so that we may benefit from them, and to be full of zeal for God and of compassion for the souls of men. A man may preach every day of the week and never have his heart affected once. This is the cause of the loss of powerful preaching in the country and of the setting up of quaint orations instead, for the providers of such talks never seek for experience in their own hearts. So it has come to pass that the preaching of some men and the lack of preaching of others, have lost us the power of what we call the ministry. Though there may be twenty or thirty thousand men in orders, yet the nation perishes for lack of knowledge. It is overwhelmed by all kinds of sins and is still today not delivered from them.

4. *Skill to divide the word correctly* is necessary. This skill to expound the word is practical wisdom in the handling of the word of God: to preach from it not only what is nourishing food for the souls of men, but what is the most appropriate food for those to whom we preach.

5. And this requires the *knowledge of the state of our flocks*, accompanied by deep reflection. A man who does not have

the state of his flock continually before his eyes and in his mind, while in his work of preaching, fights uncertainly like a man beating the air. If he is not thinking of the state of his flock with respect to temptations, to their light or their darkness, to their growth or their decay, to their flourishing or their withering, to the measure of their knowledge and attainments, he never preaches appropriately to them.

6. It is also necessary that we should be *motivated by zeal* for the glory of God, and by compassion for the souls of men.

Having delivered these few plain words, I might say: 'Who is sufficient for these things?' It is necessary to have that spiritual wisdom in order to understand the mysteries of the gospel, that ability to instruct and lead on to perfection the most mature in our congregations; that authority which proceeds from unction and is an evidence of an anointing with the graces and gifts of the Spirit (the only source of authority in preaching); that experience which conforms our whole soul into every sermon we preach, so as to feel the truth in its power; that skill by which to divide the word rightly; etc. We see therefore the great need to pray for ourselves, and that you should pray for us. Pray for your ministers. This, then, is the first duty of gospel ministers.

Second: Another duty that is required is *continual prayer for the churches* over which Christ has made you overseers. I do not have time to confirm these things by specific testimonies: you know how often the apostle mentions this of himself and presses upon others to be continually praying for the flock.

I will give four reasons why we ought to do so, and four things we ought to pray for:

(a) My first reason is that I believe that no man can have any evidence in his own soul that he is conscientiously performing any ministerial duty towards his flock, if he is not *continually praying for them*. However much he preaches, however much he visits, however much he converses, unless God keeps him in a spirit of prayer for his flock in his private prayers and with his family, he can have no evidence that he is performing any other ministerial duty appropriately, or that what he is doing is acceptable to God. I speak to those who are wise and understand these things.

(b) This is the way in which we may bless our congregations. Authoritative blessing, as far as I know, is taken from us. What is left to us is that which is expressive of our desire and is declarative, not authoritative. There is no way now by which we can bring blessing upon our flock by an authoritative form or institution. We can only *continually pray* for a blessing upon them.

(c) I do not believe that any minister, any pastor in the world, can maintain a proper love for his church if he does not pray for them. He will meet with so many provocations, follies and injuries that nothing will be able to maintain a warm love in his heart towards them without continual prayer on their behalf. Such prayer will conquer all prejudices.

(d) My last reason is this: it is in our prayers for our people that *God will teach us what we should preach to them*. We cannot pray for them without thinking beforehand what it is we should pray for, and this necessarily involves us in thinking of their situation. By this means, God teaches the ministers of the gospel. I understand that such and such is the flock's situation; I learn, therefore, what it is I should teach them. The more we pray for them, the better instructed we shall be in what to preach to them. The apostles, in order to teach us to concentrate our attentions, 'gave themselves to prayer and the word' (Acts 6:4). Prayer is noted first. This is not personal prayer but ministerial prayer for the church and for the progress of the gospel.

What should we pray for?

1. For the *success of the word* that we preach to them. This agrees with the light of nature. We are to pray for the success of the word in all its intentions; that is, in all the ways of living for God: for direction in duty; for instruction in the truth; for growth in grace; for all things by which to come to the enjoyment of God. We should pray that all these things might be fulfilled in our congregations by the proclaiming of the word, otherwise we are sowing seed at random. Seed does not grow just because it is sown; if the farmer should first break up the fallow ground and harrow it before sowing they would still have no crop unless the showers came. Similarly, after we have cast the seed of the gospel, though the hearts of men have been prepared to some degree, unless the showers of the Spirit come upon them there will be no profiting. Let us pray, therefore, that a blessing might be upon the word. Do you as a minister wish to preach, and to preach acceptably? Then learn the secret of it: pray over it. This is the only way to have our

words accepted in the people's hearts – to follow it up with prayer.

2. We are to pray for *the presence of Christ* in all our gatherings, for it is on this that all the efficacy of the ordinances of the gospel depends. Christ has given us many promises of this and we are to act in faith with respect to them, and to pray in faith for our gatherings. This is a great ministerial duty. If we do not do it, we are ignorant of our duty, and are willing to labour in the fire, where everyone perishes. We put ourselves at risk, for the effectiveness of the ordinances of preaching and praying do not depend on anything in ourselves, on our gifts, thoughts, abilities, zeal, but only on the presence of Christ. Make it your business to pray powerfully for this for your congregation, that all these might be made effectual.

3. Our prayers should be with respect to *the state and condition* of the church. Suppose that a minister is satisfied that he has some degree of understanding and knowledge in the mysteries of the gospel; that he is able to lead the best of the congregation to salvation; that he knows their measure, their weakness and their temptations; that he knows the times and seasons when they are vulnerable and under pressure, whether under adversity or under prosperity; that, as far as possible, he knows their personal situations. We then should fit our prayers according to all what we know of them, and trust in prayer that Christ himself will come in to recover those who are fallen, to establish those who stand, to heal those who backslide, to strengthen those who are tempted, to encourage those who are running and pressing forward to maturity, to relieve those who are discouraged

and in the dark – and we have all of these in our churches. Our prayers should be for a continual communication of supplies to them, in all cases.[3]

Third: Men who are pastors and teachers of churches are obliged *to preserve the truth and doctrine of the gospel* that is committed to the church: to maintain it in its entirety and defend it against all opposition. Consider the solemn words by which the apostle commits this charge to Timothy: 'O Timothy, guard the deposit entrusted to you' (1 Tim. 6:20), and 'Guard the good deposit entrusted to you' (2 Tim. 1:14). 'The good deposit – that good store, that good treasure) that has been committed to you, keep it by the help of the Holy Spirit who dwells in us.' This charge is given to all of us who are ministers: '*Keep the truth*, that good, that blessed thing.' 'It is the glorious gospel of the blessed God with which I have been entrusted,' says the apostle (1 Tim. 1:11). And it is committed to *all* our trust, and we are to keep it against all opposition. The church is the pillar and buttress of the truth, to hold it up and declare it, in and by its ministers. But is that all? No! The church is also 'like the tower of David, built in rows of stone; on it hang a thousand shields, all of them shields of warriors' (Song of Sol. 4:4). Ministers of the gospel are shields and bucklers to defend the truth against all adversaries and opposition. The church has had thousands of bucklers and shields of mighty men, otherwise the truth would have been lost. They are not only to declare it in the preaching of the gospel, but to defend and preserve it against all

[3] Albeit Owen had mentioned 'four things we ought to pray for,' the fourth seems to have been omitted.

who attack it: to hold up the shield of faith against all who assault it.

What does this involve?

(a) This requires a *clear apprehension* of those doctrines and truths which we are to defend. Truth may be lost by weakness as well as by wickedness. If we do not have a full apprehension of the truth, based on scriptural arguments and principles, we shall never be able to defend it. This must be arrived at by all ways and means – especially by means of diligent prayer and study – so that we may be able to stop the mouths of all who oppose.

(b) It requires a *love for the truth*. We shall never contend for the faith, we shall never 'buy it and not sell it,' whatever we might know of it, unless our love and respect for it arise from a sense and experience of it in our own souls. I fear that there is much loss of truth, not for want of light, knowledge and ability, but for want of love.

I have an advantage over most here present in this, in that I know the fight we had for the truths of the gospel before our troubles began, and was engaged in it from the beginning. I knew those godly ministers who contended for them as for their own lives and souls, and I saw that all the opposition made against them was never able to discourage them. What were these doctrines? They were the doctrines of eternal predestination, of effectual conversion to God and of the hardening of wicked reprobates by the providence of God. These truths are not lost for lack of skill but for lack of love. We hardly hear a word of them. We are almost ashamed to mention them in the church, and whoever does mention them can be certain of exposing himself to public abuse and scorn, but we must never be ashamed of the truth. In previous years, you could not meet a godly minister who would not consider the error of Arminianism as the ruin and poison of men's souls. Such men would write and dispute against it. But now, this is not the case. The doctrine of the gospel is still acknowledged today, though little noticed by some among ourselves. Love for it has dwindled greatly; its sense and power have been almost lost. But we have gained no ground by this. We are not more holy, more fruitful, than we were when preaching those doctrines and gathering diligently to hear them.

(c) Let us watch ourselves carefully for any tendency to *new opinions*, especially in, or about, or against those points of faith in which they who have gone before us and have fallen asleep found such life, comfort and power. Who would have thought that we would have become indifferent with respect to the doctrine of justification, and should quarrel and dispute about the merit of works in justification; indifferent as to general redemption, that belief which removes the efficacy of the redeeming work of Christ; and about the perseverance of the saints? These truths were the soul and life of those who have gone before us, those who knew the life and comfort of them. We shall not maintain these truths unless we find the same comfort in them as they did. I have lived to see great alterations in the godly ministers of the nation both in their zeal in, and their respect for, those important truths that were the life of the Reformation. Bound in at the end of their Bibles was a prayer condemning free will. But by now free will is considered an indifferent thing, and the horrible corruptions that we have allowed to be introduced into the doctrine of justification have weakened all the essential principles of religion. Let us, for the remainder of our days, 'buy truth and not sell it' (Prov. 23:23), and let us be zealous and watchful over anything that might arise in our congregations.

If you allow one man into the congregation who has a different opinion, he will raise more talk over it than all the rest of the congregation in their endeavours to build up one another in their most holy faith. Beware lest there be any men arising from among us and speaking perverse things: this is to open the way for fierce wolves to come in who will not spare the flock.

(d) *Skill and ability* is required to discover, oppose and defeat the cunning arguments of adversaries. Great prayer, watchfulness and diligence are needed that we may be able to attend to such things. Those who are less skilled would do well to be advised by others more experienced in them, for help and assistance.

Lastly: I shall mention one more duty that is required by pastors and teachers in the church, and that is: that *we labour diligently for the conversion of souls*. This work is committed to them. I mention this in order to correct the mistake made by some. The purpose of all individual churches is the calling and building up of the universal catholic church. Christ has not called his ministers to look after themselves alone: they are to be the means of calling and gathering the elect in all ages, and they do this predominantly by their ministry. I acknowledge that there are other external ways and means by which men have been, and may yet be, converted. I have found, after long experience, that a general enlightenment, together with afflictions, sometimes begin the conversions of many, without this or that particular word; and people are sometimes converted to God by personal conversation. There may be many *occasional* conversions brought about by the instrumentality of men who have real spiritual gifts for declaring the word, and who are sometimes called to exercise them.[4] But it is a work predominantly committed to the pastors of churches, for the conversion of souls.

Consider this observation: the *first object* of the word is *the world*. Our *work* is the same as that of the apostles, though our *method* is directly opposite to theirs. The apostles had a work committed to them. Their first work was the convincing and converting of sinners to Christ from among Jews and Gentiles: to preach the gospel, to convert unbelievers. This is what they accounted their chief work. Paul thought little of the administering of the ordinance of baptism in comparison with it. 'Christ did not send me to baptize but to preach the gospel' (1 Cor. 1:17). Preaching was their first work. And then, their *second work* was to teach the disciples to do and observe all that Christ had commanded, and to bring them into a church order. This was their method. Since the days of the apostles the same work is committed to the pastors of churches, but with a different method. The first object of our ministry is the church: building up and edifying the church. But does this mean that the other part of the work is not required – preaching to convert souls? God forbid. There are several ways by which pastors of churches do preach to the conversion of souls:

[4] Owen is referring here to lay-preachers.

(a) When unconverted people attend their churches (which we experience daily) and on hearing their sermons to their congregations are converted to God by this fulfilling of pastoral duty. 'This is not the case,' say some. 'They are preaching as *ministers* only to the church, to the others they speak only as men who are spiritually gifted.' But no one makes this distinction in his own conscience. Imagine that there were five hundred present here of which one hundred were members of the church. Would you make the distinction, would you view me as preaching in a double capacity: to some as a minister and to others not as a minister? There is no rule or reason behind such a thought. We preach as ministers to those to whom we preach, for the conversion of their souls.

(b) Ministers may preach for the conversion of souls when they preach occasionally away from their own churches. They preach as ministers wherever they preach. I know that 'the *indelible character*'[5] is a figment, but the pastor's office is not something that men can leave at home when they travel. It is not in a minister's own power, unless he has been lawfully dismissed, to stop himself from preaching as a minister. And it is the duty of individual churches (because one purpose of their existence is the calling and gathering together of the universal catholic church) to part with their officers for a time, when these are called to preach in some other place in order to convert souls to Christ. We had a

[5] The 'indelible character' is the dogma of the church of Rome: that a man ordained to be a priest within its pale can never lose his priestly character. Though he may cease to be a Christian, he cannot cease from being a Christian bishop, priest or deacon, if he has previously held any of these offices in the church.—G.

glorious ministry in the previous age: wonderful instruments for the conversion of souls. Did these convert people only as gifted men rather than as ministers? God forbid. I have said that this may be the experience of some who have received gifts, but not been called to office, but I do not know of any justification for a man who has committed himself to the ministry, not to say, in prayer, 'Lord, here I am; send me.'

Had I time and strength I would tell you of the duty of pastors and teachers in administering the seals, and of what this requires; I would mention the duty of directing and comforting the consciences of all sorts of believers: the wisdom, purity, humility and patience that is needed in this, a major part of our work as pastors.

I would show you also the role of pastors in the rule of the church. Not that Christ ever intended to commit the rule of the church to them alone: this would take them from the great and important duty of preaching the gospel; but as time and circumstances allow them they must give their attention to ruling the church.

Lastly, I would speak of their responsibility to be examples of godly behaviour, and of the need to meet with other churches holding to the same beliefs, so as to maintain good fellowship between churches.

'Who is sufficient for these things?' Pray, pray for us. And may God strengthen us, and our brother who has been called today to the work! May it not have been unprofitable for him, and for myself, to have been reminded of these things, and to pray for help from our brothers.

Sermon 6

The Nature and Beauty of Gospel Worship

*For through him we both have access in one Spirit to the
Father*—Eph. 2:18

In the previous verses the apostle refers to a double reconciliation wrought by the blood of the cross. The first is the
reconciliation of Jews and Gentiles to God; the second of
Jews and Gentiles to one another. There were two things
upheld in the law: firstly, the worship which was instituted
under it; secondly, the curse annexed to it. In that the first
of these was committed to the Jews, with the Gentiles
being excluded, it was the cause of great enmity and hatred
between them. The latter, the curse, fell on both of them, and
was the cause of the enmity between them both and God.
The Lord Jesus Christ, in his removal of both of these by his
death, effected the twofold reconciliation mentioned. First,
he broke down 'the dividing wall of hostility' and 'made
us both one' (verse 14), that is, both Jews and Gentiles. He
has taken away every cause for any difference which might
obstruct our oneness in him. How has he done this? By
taking away 'the law of commandments and ordinances'

(verse 15); that is, by abolishing that particular worship which was the Jews' privilege and burden, and from which the Gentiles were excluded. In this way the dividing wall was broken down. Secondly, by his death on the cross, he 'killed the hostility,' he took away the curse of the law, thereby reconciling both Jews and Gentiles to God (verse 16). By bearing the curse of the law he reconciled both to God, and by taking away and abolishing the worship of the law he removed all causes of difference between them.

From this reconciliation there results a twofold advantage or privilege: *firstly*, an access into God's favour, who previously was at enmity with both; *secondly*, a new and more glorious way of approaching God in worship than the previous manner, which had set them so much apart.

The first of these is mentioned in Romans 5:2, and what is there termed 'access by faith into this grace in which we stand' may be identified in our text with 'access to the Father'; that is, the favour and acceptance with God which we enjoy. Our access to God is that sense of acceptance we have based on the reconciliation made for us by Jesus Christ. However, I do not believe that this is the main emphasis in our text. Rather, the main thought is of that access to God which is the effect of the reconciliation of Jews and Gentiles by the abolishing of the ceremonial law. A new and more glorious way of worship, provided for them both, is being described. Before the reconciliation was made, only one party had the privilege of the external, ceremonial worship that had been instituted, but now both parties enjoy a form of worship which provides for them an immediate access to God. The apostle here asserts the beauty and glory of the new gospel worship of both Jew and Gentile as being above that previously enjoyed by the Jew: that worship which had been a matter of separation and division between them.

This would appear to be the meaning of verse 17. What is being described is not an immediate result of the reconciliation effected by the blood of Christ upon the cross, but of his preaching of peace and of his calling of both Jews and Gentiles: gathering them to himself and, therefore, to the worship of God. Being called by the word of peace to worship, both Jew and Gentile, we now have this access.

The words following, to the end of the chapter, make this all the more evident. The apostle discusses many things that are now true of the Gentiles because of this access to God.

Firstly, negatively, they are no longer 'strangers and aliens' (verse 19); that is, they are not so with respect to the worship of God, though this was their case before being reconciled and called. The apostle had described them as 'the uncircumcision,' 'alienated' and 'strangers' (verses 11, 12); that is, men who had no share in, or admittance to, the solemn worship of God confined to the commonwealth of Israel. 'But this is no longer the case,' he says; that is, you have a share and an interest in that worship by which God is well pleased.

Secondly, positively, Paul affirms two things that are true of them: They are 'fellow citizens with the saints and members of the household of God' (verse 19). They are being built up into 'a holy temple' or 'a dwelling place for God' (verses 20-22). Both these things relate to the solemn worship of God under the gospel. The first testifies to their now being members of the church; the second, to the fact that by

them, and among them, God was being worshipped with
that divine service which had replaced the temple worship
that Christ had taken away.

As this is the meaning of the Holy Spirit in this passage,
I shall present it as one proposition to you.

*Observation: It is a pre-eminent effect and fruit of our
reconciliation to God and among ourselves, by the blood of
Christ, that believers enjoy the privileges of the excellent,
glorious and spiritual worship of God in Christ, as revealed
and required in the gospel.*

In expounding this text, I shall:

I. Prove, briefly, that we obtain this privilege as a fruit,
and on account of, the reconciliation made by the blood of
Christ.

II. Show that the worship of the gospel is indeed so
beautiful, glorious and excellent that the enjoyment of it is
a great privilege.

I. I shall confirm that *believers enjoy this privilege as a fruit
and effect of the death and blood of Jesus Christ* by referring only to one or two texts. Compare, for example, two
passages in the Epistle to the Hebrews 9:8 and 10:19-22.
Whilst the first tabernacle was standing, before Christ by
his death had removed it and the worship that accompanied it (the dividing wall that he broke down), there was no
immediate admission to God. The way into the holy places
not made with hands, which we now make use of, was not
yet opened; the worshippers were kept at a great distance,
making their application to God by outward, ceremonial
ordinances (Heb. 9:8). Once the tabernacle was removed,

a way was opened into the holiest for the worshippers. How is that obtained? By what means? It is 'by the blood of Jesus Christ,' by the rending of his flesh (Heb. 10:19). This privilege of entering into the holiest, which is a true description of all gospel worship, could not be obtained or granted to believers by any other way but by the blood of Christ. We 'enter the holiest place by the blood of Christ,' by which he prepared, perfected, or 'opened for us … a new and living way' (verse 20). Peter gives us a similar account of the obtaining of this privilege: believers offer up 'spiritual sacrifices acceptable to God through Jesus Christ' (1 Pet. 2:4, 5). This is the worship which we are considering. To make them fit for this worship and capable of performing it they are made 'a spiritual house' and 'a holy priesthood' (verse 5). They are made both the temple in which God dwells by his Spirit, and the priests that offer acceptable sacrifices to him. By what means, then, have they obtained this honour? By 'coming to him' as he was, 'rejected by men, but in the sight of God, chosen and precious' (verse 4). By this phrase, the apostle includes the whole mystery of Christ's death and shedding of blood, in which he was very publicly rejected by men, and most gloriously owned of God, when he acknowledged Christ's fulfilling of the work of reconciliation.

Leaving the first part of the observation and proceeding to the second:

II. *The worship of God under the gospel is so excellent, beautiful and glorious, that it must be esteemed a privilege, purchased by the blood of Christ, which no man can truly and really possess other than by virtue of an interest in the reconciliation worked by Christ.* For 'through him we both have access in one Spirit to the Father.'

I shall show this in two ways:—first, *Absolutely*; and secondly, *Comparatively*, with reference to any other way of worshipping.

FIRST, It is a principle that is deeply fixed in men's minds, indeed, engrafted into them by nature, that the worship of God ought to be orderly, seemly, beautiful and glorious. Therefore, throughout the ages, men who have seen it as their responsibility to imagine, discover, and frame the worship of God, or anything belonging to it, have always sought out things which, in themselves or in their use, are, in their judgment, beautiful, comely, orderly and glorious. Any worship which comes short of these properties may well be suspected of not being in accordance with the mind of God. I must add one obvious qualification, which no one could reasonably deny, that God himself is the most proper judge of the case. If, therefore, we are not convinced that spiritual gospel worship, in its own naked simplicity, without any other added external help or decoration, is the most orderly, seemly, beautiful and glorious form (the Holy Spirit in the Scripture being the judge), we will wish to look out for these other helps from other (alleged) sources.

1. The first thing, in general, found in these words is that in the spiritual worship of the gospel the three persons of the blessed Trinity engage in distinct communion with the souls of the worshippers. The Trinity as a whole, and each person of the Trinity individually, in that economy and dispensation by which they act, severally and specifically, in the work of our redemption, are engaged in this communion. We find them mentioned distinctly in the text: 'Through him' (that is, Jesus Christ, the Son of God)

'we have access in one Spirit' (that good and Holy Spirit) 'to the Father' (a title which must be taken hypostatically or 'personally,' when used in distinction from the Son and the Spirit). There is no act, part or duty of gospel worship in which the worshippers do not have this distinct communion with each person of the blessed Trinity.[1] We shall return to a more detailed discussion of this later.

The text provides the general order of gospel worship, the great rubric, the directions for our divine service. Here, in general, is found the propriety of our worship, in its respect of the mediation of the Son, through whom we have access; the supplies and assistance of the Spirit; and a regard to God as a Father. He who fails in any one of these, breaks all order in gospel worship. If we do not approach it by Jesus Christ, or do not fulfil it in the strength of the Holy Spirit, or do not go to God as Father in it, we transgress all the rules of this worship. This is the great canon, which, if it is neglected, will ensure that there is no decency in whatever else is done. And this, in general, is the glory of our worship. Worship is certainly an act of the soul (Matt. 22:37). The body has its share by its accompaniment and obedience to the directions of the mind. The actions of body and mind receive their elevation and glory from the object with whom they are engaged. That object, in this gospel worship, is God himself, in his Son and Holy Spirit, and no other. Acting faith in Christ for admission; and on the Holy Spirit for his help (so that we proceed in his strength); and on God, even the Father, for acceptance: this is the work of the soul in this

[1] This theme is discussed in a lengthy treatise by Owen: 'On Communion with God the Father, Son, and Holy Ghost,' *Works*, vol. 2 (London: Banner of Truth Trust, 1965), pp. 1-274.

worship. I have yet to learn of anything more glorious with which it can be engaged. But these things will be discussed later. In general, they define the order and glory of the worship which we are considering.

2. The same point is true from its general nature: that it is an access to God. 'Through him we have access to the Father.' There are two things here that demonstrate the excellence, order and glory involved: (a) It provides an access; (b) The nature of that access, indicated by the word used in the original Greek (*prosagōgē*).

(a) It is an access, an approach, a drawing near to God. This is how the apostle describes it, 'Let us draw near with a true heart' (Heb. 10:22); that is, to God, in 'the holy places' (verse 19). When the law was first given and the accompanying worship instituted, the people were commanded to keep at a distance. They were not, on pain of death, so much as to touch the mountain where God was present (Exod. 19:12). They therefore stood far off, while Moses alone drew near to the thick darkness where God was (Exod. 20:21). Similarly, when the high priest went into the most holy place once a year with blood (to which I will refer again later), and also when the priests in their rotas went daily into the holy place to burn incense, the people were kept outside (as in Luke 1:10). But in this gospel worship we have access; we draw near to God. There is no interposition of curtains or of any other external ordinance. All has been made open and a new and living way of access given to us (Heb. 10:20). I do not know of anything further that could be added to set forth the glory of this worship to a soul who knows what it is to draw near to God. The heathens of old derided the

Egyptians who, through many imposing buildings and with most pompous ceremonies, brought their worshippers to the image of an ape. I will not say any more: but let those who design much of their worship around the ceremonial access to an altar or image consider how they will justify themselves. The plea of referring to God at the very end has been used by idolaters of all sorts, from the beginning of the world.

(b) It is a *prosagōgē* that we have in this worship: a 'manuduction' [a 'leading by the hand'] to God, in order and with much glory. It is the kind of access that men have to the presence of a king, when they are handed in by some favourite or great person. This, in gospel worship, is done by Christ. He takes the worshippers by the hand and leads them into the presence of God. He there presents them (as we shall see), saying, 'Behold, I and the children God has given me' (Heb. 2:13). This is the access of believers; this is the way that they enter into God's presence. Some, perhaps, might say that a man should be ashamed to speak such great things as these of poor worms who are not ordered in their ways, eloquent in their words, or beautiful in their worship. Let such men know that they will have to hear even greater things of them. It is only right, indeed, that these worshippers should be conformable to Christ in all things. This means that in the eyes of the world they will never have any form or majesty or beauty in themselves, in their way, or their worship (as in Isa. 53:2). 'The world does not know' them and their ways because 'it did not know him, nor his ways' (1 John 3:1). But if God may be allowed to judge his own affairs, the spiritual worship of the saints is glorious since they have in it such an access, such a leading by the hand to God.

3. The excellence and glory of this worship is seen also from its immediate object, which is God. We have an access to God. It is, as I said, the Father that is meant here particularly. God, as God – he who is the beginning and end of all things, whose nature is of infinite perfection, he from whom all sovereignty proceeds – he is the formal object of all divine and religious worship. Therefore, divine worship has respect, as its object, to each person of the blessed Trinity equally, not as this or that person, but as each person is God. This is the formal reason of all divine worship. Yet, in that the second person is considered as vested with his office of mediator, and the Holy Spirit as the helper and sanctifier of the saints, so God the Father is in a distinct manner considered the object of our faith, love and worship. Thus Peter tells us that through Christ we 'are believers in God, who raised him from the dead and gave him glory' (1 Pet. 1:21). As Christ is considered as mediator, then God, who raised him from the dead (that is, the Father), is regarded as the ultimate object of our worship; although, just as we worship him who is the Father as God, so also the other persons are worshipped as God. All this is presented in Galatians 4:6 (which I cannot deal with presently), which explains that in our access to God, Christ being considered as the mediator and the Holy Spirit as our comforter, advocate and helper, the saints have a particular respect to the person of the Father.

Two things arise from this, demonstrating the order, decency and glory of gospel worship: (a) That in worship we have a direct and immediate access to God; (b) That we have access to him as the Father of our Lord Jesus Christ and as our Father in Christ.

(a) Not the least part of the glory of this worship is that our access is to *God himself*. When outward worship was at its height and glory, the immediate access of worshippers was only to some visible sign or pledge of God's presence. The temple itself is an example; or the ark, or the mercy-seat. Paul, when he describes the worshippers of the tabernacle or the temple, therefore describes them as 'comers to sacrifices' (Heb. 10:1). There was, as it were, a barrier put up before them; they could approach, 'come to,' the visible representations of God's majesty and presence, but not proceed further. But now, in this spiritual worship of the gospel, the saints have direct and immediate access to God: the way into 'the holy places not made with hands' being laid open before them. And when they are encouraged to make use of outward signs, as in the sacraments, this is not, as it were, to stop them from entering heaven, but to help them forward through the entrance (as all who are acquainted with the true use of these sacraments are fully aware). I am not saying that any of the worship of old was limited in the sensible sense and tokens of God's presence, but only that the spirit of the worshippers was kept in subjection, in the sense that they could only approach God to the extent that he exhibited himself to their faith in those signs, and not immediately as we do under the gospel.

(b) In this spiritual worship of the gospel we have access to God *as Father*. I showed, at the beginning, that God is distinctly presented to us here as the Father of our Lord

Jesus Christ, and in him, as our God and Father. We are therefore said to come 'to the throne of grace' (Heb. 4:16); that is, to God as he is gloriously exalted in the dispensation of grace, in kindness, love and mercy: in a word, as a Father. God on the throne of grace, and God as a Father, are one and the same. As a Father, he is all love, grace and mercy to his children in Christ. When God came of old to institute his worship in the giving of the law, he did it with the dreadful and terrible representation of his majesty, so that the people feared to come near but went and 'stood far off, and said to Moses, "You speak to us, and we will listen; but do not let God speak to us, lest we die"' (Exod. 20:18, 19). And by this dreadful representation of the majesty of God, as the object of their worship, they were kept in fear and bondage all their days. But now the saints are encouraged to approach God as a Father. The glory of this is described wonderfully by the apostle (Rom. 8:18, 19). That fear and slavery in which men were kept under the law has now been removed and in its place the spirit of children, approaching their father with reverent boldness, is given to us. This, I say, adds to the glory, beauty and excellence of gospel worship. The weakest believer, with his broken prayers and requests, still has an immediate access to God, and to him as Father. The most despised church of saints on earth brings its worship to the glorious presence of God himself. And let me add, in passing, that the attempt to worship God by men who are not interested in this privilege of access to him, is the source of all the superstitious idolatry that is in the world. I will note two examples, from which all others spring:

(i) Not having any experience of the excellence of this privilege, or not being satisfied with it, men have turned aside to worship saints and angels in heaven. The basis for all the justifications that Papists plead for this practice is exactly this: 'That we might have access to God! It would be too presumptuous to come to him directly, so it is right and proper for us humbly to make use of the favourites of the court of heaven, of saints and angels, and ask them to entreat with God for us.' Now, quite apart from their ignorance of the work of Christ as mediator, which is plain infidelity, what they are saying amounts to this: 'We don't have any belief in gospel worship (in which believers, by Jesus Christ, have direct "access with confidence" (Eph. 3:12) to God himself), so we depend on this "voluntary humility" (as the apostle calls it, Col. 2:18, KJV; 'asceticism,' ESV), rather than risk such an approach to God.' Such is the reasoning of men who are not acquainted with this element of the glory of gospel worship.

(ii) Because they have no knowledge of a direct access to God himself, they are therefore forced to invent external, visible pledges and signs of God's presence (as imagined by them) which they may then approach. Images, icons, altars and the *east* are therefore introduced into worship, with which they may pursue an immediate conversation: their thoughts may have access to these and, by them, as they think, to God. For the same reason the sacraments must be changed and what was provided to help us in our entrance to God is itself made a god, so that men may have easy access to him. Carnal men, who know nothing of the spiritual, whose souls are not in any way moulded and affected by pure acts of faith, are here stirred by their senses, and use these additions in their performance of worship. And this is the basis from which has developed all the pompous ceremonies invented by men for God's worship. It is just a device and invention to provide carnally-minded men with something to pass as worship, not having any principle that enables them to make use of this privilege of approaching God himself.

4. The glory of gospel worship is seen again in the principal cause and means of our access to God, namely, Jesus Christ. It is through him that we have this access. This is a further source of beauty and glory in worship, and its elements must be considered. That access which the people of God had in the past to the outward pledge of God's presence was by their high priest; not in his own person but solely by his representation of them. And this access occurred only once a year. But in the worship of the gospel the saints have an access through Christ to God himself, in their own persons, and continually. We have this access in Christ for many reasons:

(a) Because *he has purchased and obtained this favour for us* so that we might approach God and find favour with him. We are 'accepted in the Beloved' (Eph. 1:6, KJV). I cannot give the time to show how by paying a ransom for us and 'bearing our iniquities' he has answered the law, removed the curse, reconciled us to God, pacified his anger, satisfied justice, and obtained for us an eternal redemption. All this is involved in his obtaining this favour of acceptance with God. The apostle summates it: Christ has, as a high priest, made 'propitiation for the sins of the people' (Heb. 2:17).

Because of this they have 'access by faith into this grace' (Rom. 5:2). It is in this sense that our access to God is through Christ. He has purchased it for us. It is not the least part of the price of his blood. Nothing else could have bought it; not all the wealth of the world, not all the worth of the angels in heaven; nothing could do it except Christ himself. Go into the most opulent, impressive place of outward worship upon earth; consider all the wealth and glory of its structure and ornaments. A wise man, perhaps, might estimate what it all cost, what its value is. However, even the most foolish could tell you that all it cost was money. It was bought with 'silver and gold' and 'perishable things,' it is the 'thick clay' (Hab. 2:6, KJV), and it is the wealthiest person who can produce the most beautiful and most glorious of that kind of worship. But the gospel worship of believers is the price of 'the blood of the Son of God.' Access for sinners to God could not be obtained by any other way. Let men 'lavish gold from the purse' upon their idols, as the prophet says (Isa. 46:6); their self-invented worship will come as far short, in true glory and beauty, of the weakest prayers of poor saints, as the fruit of perishable things does of the fruit of the blood and death of the Son of God (1 Pet. 1:18, 19).

(b) We have this access from Christ into the presence of God *because he has opened, prepared and dedicated a way for us to enter*. Though favour may have been obtained, a way to enter must also be provided; otherwise poor souls might say, 'There is indeed water in the well; but the well is deep and we have nothing to draw water with. There is an acceptance purchased for us in God's presence, but by what way shall we come to him?' Christ has also provided a way for us by which we may enter: 'A new and living way' (Heb. 10:19, 20). In the past, the way into the holiest place was through the curtain that hung before it, which the apostle called 'the second curtain' (Heb. 9:3). Its description and function is given in Exodus 26:31-35. Through this curtain the high priest entered into the holiest place. But for an entrance into the presence of God in the holiest place not made with hands, Christ has provided and dedicated a 'new and living way' for us. This way is himself. He told Thomas, 'I am the way' (John 14:6). It is only by him that anyone can obtain an access to God.

In our continual approach in worship there is constant reference to Christ's suffering for us in the flesh. We enter 'by his blood' and 'through his flesh.' Why is this? Just as men, approaching some great potentate or general, have a password or token which they show, or make use of, if any try to stop their approach, so it is with believers. The law would stop them in their access to God; so would sin and Satan; but being 'sprinkled with the blood of Christ' is the token that opens everything before them and removes all obstacles. And when in the presence of God, it is the suffering of Christ in the flesh that they depend on for their acceptance. They go to God through him, in his name, 'making mention of his righteousness' (Psa. 71:16, KJV), his death and the shedding of his blood, pleading for acceptance on his account. This is their new and living way for going to God; this is the path they tread, the entrance they use. No man may obtain access to God unless he knows this way. I am not at all surprised that those who are ignorant of it, who have no share of it, nor ever took one step upon it, will commit themselves to any other kind of worship whatsoever, rather than experiencing for once what it is to place the glory of their worship in an access to God, for they have no portion or part in this way, and without that, any attempt is fruitless and vain.

All this adds to the order, and increases the glory and beauty, of the spiritual worship of the gospel. Go to the mass-book and its rubric. You will see there how many instructions and directions are given to the priests about the way of entering their sanctum and approaching their altars: how they must bow and bend themselves, sometimes one way, sometimes another; sometimes kneel, sometimes stand, sometimes go forwards, sometimes backward. This is their way to their bread-god. This is what they call order, beauty and glory, and with such things are poor, simple souls deluded and carnal wretches, enemies to Christ and his Spirit, blinded to their eternal ruin. Surely, I believe, the gospel way of approach to God is far more reverent and glorious. It is in and by Christ; a way purposefully dedicated by him. It was opened by his suffering in the flesh and abides a new and living way for ever. If men were not so utterly blind, if they were not so incapable of seeing anything afar off, if they were not so wholly carnal and unspiritual, 'not setting their minds on the things of God,' it would seem impossible that they should reject these pearls of the gospel for the husks of swine, such things that are worse even than the ways of the old heathens. The only thing that can be said to excuse them is that they throw away and reject that in which they have no part, in preference for that which is very properly their own.

(c) We have this access through Christ in that he has entered before us into the presence of God *to make a way for our access to him*, and our acceptance with him. According to the apostle, 'We have a great high priest who has passed through the heavens, Jesus, the Son of God' (Heb. 4:14). He has already gone into God's presence for that purpose. The same apostle tells us, 'Let us look "behind the curtain, where Jesus has gone as a forerunner on our behalf"' (Heb. 6:19, 20). He is a forerunner for us; one who has gone in to the presence of God to declare that all his saints are coming to him, coming into his presence with their solemn worship and prayers. He has entered heaven to carry the news, as it were, and to make way for the entrance of his saints. This is great encouragement for us to follow him. He has gone before us and is continually waiting for the coming of those for whom he is the forerunner. For those to whom Christ is precious and honourable, this adds to the glory of gospel worship. As for those by whom he is despised, it is no wonder that they despise his way also.

A further matter that is also part of the rubric of gospel worship and adds to its glory, is that the access to the Father in the holiest places not made with hands is on the basis of the atonement made, and the favour and acceptance purchased by Jesus Christ. This atonement, bought by the sprinkling of his blood, accompanied him as he went before us to provide admittance for us. Here also is order and beauty, if we have either eyes or faith to perceive beauty.

(d) We have this access through Christ *because he is 'the high priest over the house of God.'* How much the apostle emphasizes this in the Epistle to the Hebrews. One or two examples will be sufficient to show this. In Hebrews 4:14-16, the inference drawn from the fact that Christ our high priest has entered heaven is that we should approach the throne of grace; and because he is such a high priest as is described here, we should approach with confidence of our acceptance with God. This is the theme that the apostle deals with generally throughout the epistle. However great the outward glory and splendour of the worship associated with the law, yet that which is appointed in the gospel is to be much preferred, in that the gospel's high priest is so far above the high priest who administered the former. Again, in Hebrews 10:21, 22, the encouragement to draw near to God is taken from the fact that we have 'a great priest over the house of God.' That which the Holy Spirit requires of those who draw near to worship God, under the guidance and leadership of this blessed and merciful high priest, is also significant. Is it that they should be wearing the appropriate vestments and ornaments as they approach? No! But that they should be clothed with faith, sanctification and holiness. These are the three great qualifications of gospel worshippers. 'Let us draw near,' he says, 'with a true heart in full assurance of faith, with our hearts sprinkled clean from an evil conscience and our bodies washed with pure water'; that is, purified by the blood of Christ, typified in baptism; or it refers, perhaps, to being effectually cleansed in soul and body by the Holy Spirit, who, in the work of purifying and sanctifying the souls of believers, is often compared to water.

I wish to give some time to this general point, in order to demonstrate further the beauty, order and glory of the spiritual worship of God as it consists in our access to him through Christ, the 'great high priest over the house of God.' It is indeed so great, that the apostle makes it the conclusion of his whole argument with respect to the excellence of the gospel, and our approach to God by it. 'The point we are saying is this,' he says. 'those of old had a high priest, and a ministry performed by him, which comprised the glory of their worship. We also have a high priest, but there is no comparison between ours and theirs.' He then proceeds to describe him. Firstly, in terms of his dignity, honour and glory: He is 'seated at the right hand of the throne of the Majesty in heaven.' Secondly, in terms of his office or ministry: He does not minister in a tabernacle, like that of Moses or of Solomon's temple, but in heaven itself, the place of the glorious presence and immediate manifestation of God's glory, which he calls 'the true tent that the Lord set up'; that is, which God appointed for the place of worship for his saints under the ministry of Christ, their high priest (Heb. 8:1, 2). And although other places are necessary here on earth for their assemblies, in that they are men, clothed in flesh and weakness, yet there are none pitched, appointed and consecrated for the holy and solemn acceptance of their service, other than heaven itself. As far as the assemblies here below are concerned, all places are now alike. And what can be more glorious than this: that all the spiritual worship of the gospel, proffered here on earth by the saints, is administered in heaven by such a holy Priest, who is at the right hand of the throne of the Majesty of God! In addition, under his direction, we have also an entrance by faith into God's presence.

Away then, you who despise the spiritual worship of the gospel; you that say that unless it is adorned (or rather, in reality, defiled) by rites and ceremonies of your own invention, it has no order, reverence or beauty in it! Unite in finding out whatever pleases your imagination; borrow this from the Jews, the other from the Pagans, everything of the Papists, that you think will meet your purpose; pour out gold from the bag in order to beautify it. Do you think that it will then compare with this glory of the worship of the gospel, conducted and administered by this glorious high priest? It may be that they will say that they have this also, and that their ornaments do not devalue it, that their worship also has the glory that belongs to the attendance of the high priest. But do they really believe so? Valuing it as little as they seem to do? Why are they not content with true gospel worship, instead of finding many inventions of their own to help it along? Surely, it is impossible that men who are thoroughly convinced of its spiritual excellence should fall into that conceit of believing that they can make additions of their own to it. Nor do they seem to understand clearly that the holy God has continually contrasted this spiritual excellence of gospel worship to the outward splendour of rites and ordinances, which he himself had instituted for a period. What men therefore attempt to add on, serves only to diminish true worship. One day it will be known by all whether it is the lack of spiritual excellence in the ministry of gospel worship conducted by the glorious high priest, or the lack of minds enlightened to discern it and hearts quickened to experience it, which causes some to lay all the weight of the beauty of gospel worship on elements that they discover for themselves or that they borrow from others who were blind with regard to all spiritual communion with God in Christ. But if anyone is inclined to be contentious, 'we have no such practice, nor do the churches of God.' I only hope that it will not one day be accounted a crime that some will follow their consciences, and be content with that glory and beauty, in their worshipping of God, given to them by an access to God by Jesus Christ, as the great high priest of their profession and service.

It is an inexpressible encouragement and comfort to all the saints, in their duty of drawing near to God, whether personally, in families, or in assemblies, that Jesus Christ is the great high priest who admits them to God's presence: he who is the minister of that heavenly tabernacle where God is worshipped by them. If we are able to look to the things that are unseen, as the apostle speaks (2 Cor. 4:18) – that is, with eyes of faith – we will find that glory which will give us rest and satisfaction. For others we may pray, as Elisha did for his servant, that the Lord would open their eyes, and they would quickly see the poor, undefended places of the saints' assemblies attended not only by horses and chariots of fire, but also by Christ walking in the midst of them in that glory by which he is described (Rev. 1:13-16). And all their painted and carved images will surely come short of this. And if Christ Jesus is pleased, in his inexpressible love, to call his churches and ministers his 'glory,' as he does (2 Cor. 8:23), surely they may be content in making him their only glory.

On this last point we may observe:

(i) Our Saviour warned us of some who thought they would be heard because of their 'empty phrases' and 'many words' (Matt. 6:7). I won't apply this to any, but will say this, that men are greatly mistaken if they think they will be heard for their unspiritual, self-invented aids to devotion. But here lies the joy and confidence of poor saints, that they have a merciful high priest over the house of God, by whom they are encouraged to draw near with confidence to the throne of grace. He takes them by the hand and leads them to God's presence, where, through his means, they obtain a favourable acceptance.

(ii) Nor need they worry with regard to their outward state and condition. This was the misery of the Jews of old: that when they were driven from Jerusalem and carried into captivity, they were deprived of all the solemn worship of God. They had no high priest, no sacrifice, no tabernacle or solemn assemblies: these had all been confined to Jerusalem. We understand therefore why David complained so bitterly when, because of Saul's persecution, he was driven for a season from the place of God's holy and solemn worship. He could not view the glorious ornaments of the high priest's vestments, or the beautiful structure of the temple, or the order of the Levites and priests in worship. It is now so different for the people of God, however poor or destitute their outward circumstances. Do they meet in the mountains, in the caves and dens of the earth? Christ, according to his promise, is among them as their high priest, and (while obeying gospel rules) they have in their worship all the order, glory and beauty that may be enjoyed in any place under heaven. All depends on the presence of Christ and their access to God by him, and he is not excluded from any place and considers any place sufficiently prepared for him if his saints are meeting, or have been driven, there. Let the hands that are hanging down be lifted up, and the feeble knees be strengthened; whatever their outward distressed condition may be, there is more order, beauty and glory here than the world can ever pretend to!

(iii) Here is spiritual encouragement for the saints with respect to the standing of their souls before God. They are given views of the glory, majesty and holiness of God. They know that he is a 'consuming fire'; they have visions of his glories, of which the world has no knowledge. They are also sensible of their own poverty, wretchedness, sin and weakness – how unfit, how unable to approach him, or to have anything to do with him in his holy worship – they are ashamed of their own prayers and requests, so that often, when they have been expressed, they wish they had never been uttered, so inappropriate they seem before the greatness and holiness of God. In such a condition there is so much relief supplied to faith by considering this high priest.

To expand on this, and to emphasize further the beauty and glory of gospel worship, let me present three more points:

First, *Our high priest bears and takes away all the sinfulness and failings that accompany the holy worship of his saints.* The world is apt to despise the worship of the saints as inferior and contemptible; unworthy of the majesty of God. This is what drives them to invent what they think is more glorious and beautiful, though God abhors it. But the saints themselves see even more defects, deficiencies and failings in their worship than the world ever sees; they know how unfit and unsuited it is to the holy majesty of God, with whom they have to do. They know how the bitter root of unbelief in their hearts springs up and defiles both them and their duties; how effectively pride works in their minds, and a secret unwillingness in their wills, during their best efforts and most solemn acts of worship. They know all the other sinful attitudes that often gain a hold and a place in their hearts. These, they know, are things that, in and of themselves, are enough to defile, pollute and render all their worship unacceptable. Indeed, if God was to note every failing, the guilt of their holy worship would be sufficient to make it, and those who offer it, rejected forever. But now, here is their relief; here, beauty, glory and order are recovered for their worship. Christ as high priest removes all the evil, filth and iniquity of their holy things, so that they may be presented pure, holy and glorious before God. Aaron, as a type, did the same (Exod. 28:38). In this way, Christ, our high priest, atones for everything that is amiss: all failings, all miscarriages in his saints, he takes to his own account. Anything, on the other hand, that is of his Spirit enters into the presence of the holy God. Christ presents it to himself, and by him it is presented to God (Eph. 5:25-27). This is how the Lord Christ preserves the glory and beauty of gospel worship, notwithstanding all the defects, failures and defilements which, from the weakness and sins of his saints, seem to cling to it.

Secondly, this is not enough. As well as the weakness, sinfulness and imperfections that affect the duties of the saints, for which they might justly be rejected, there is no merit of any kind by which they might be accepted: nothing that would be a fragrance to God. Therefore, *Christ, as the high priest by whom all believers find their access to God, takes their offerings and prayers and adds incense to them so that they may become fragrant in heaven* (Rev. 8:3). Priests offer their sacrifices of prayer at the altar, and our altar is in heaven. Other men may build their altars elsewhere, but the Lord Christ, the high priest in the temple of God in heaven, in the holy places not made with hands, is the angel who stands at the altar before the Lord, the golden altar of incense before the throne. Not at the altar for sacrifice, for that work he has completely fulfilled already, but at the altar of incense, or intercession, which is that element of his work that remains to be done. On this golden altar the prayers of the saints are offered. But how can they be acceptable to God? Because this high priest has much incense, a bottomless store and treasure of righteousness – the only sweet perfume accepted by God – that he adds to them. This makes all their worship truly glorious. Christ, the high priest, takes away their iniquities and failings, adds to their worship his own righteousness, and in his own person offers it on the golden altar (that is, he, himself) before the throne of God continually.

Just as this contributes so gloriously to the comfort of believers, so it demolishes the glory of all that outward pompous worship in which so many delight. What can comfort believers more than that the Lord Christ takes their poor weak prayers, of which they are often so ashamed, and by which they are often so humbled, and which they themselves are ready to condemn, and to them adds the incense of his own righteousness, making them acceptable at the throne of grace! They have very little appreciation of the beauty and glory by which their offerings, which so trouble them, are clothed. As for the self-invented rites of men, how much does a single thought, in faith, of this ministry of Christ in heaven, cast contempt and shame upon them! What is all their gaudy dispositions when compared to the high priest of the saints offering up their prayers on the golden altar before the throne of God? This is true order, comeliness and beauty.

Thirdly, Christ, as the high priest of the saints, *presents both their persons and their duties in the presence of, and before, the Lord.* This is what was typified of old by the precious stones set in gold on the breast and shoulders of the high priest, with the names of the children of Israel upon them (Exod. 28:21). Christ, our high priest, has entered into the holy places for us, and there presents all his saints and their worship before the Lord, being 'not ashamed to call them brothers,' and saying of them, 'Behold, I and the children God has given me' (Heb. 2:11, 13).

This was the fourth point from these words manifesting the excellence and glory of gospel worship and deriving from that one great source: that it is an access to God, *through Christ.*

Sermon 7

The Nature and Beauty of Gospel Worship (cont.)

'For through him we both have access in one Spirit to the Father.'—Eph. 2:18

5. IT also adds greatly to the glory and excellence of evangelical worship that we have this access to God 'in one Spirit,' or 'by one Spirit.'

I shall show briefly: (1) How we have this access 'in the Spirit'; and (2) how we have it 'in one Spirit.'

(1) It is not questioned by any that it is the Holy Spirit who is being referred to here. He is that 'one and the same Spirit' who works in these things and who 'apportions to each one individually as he wills' (1 Cor. 12:11). I shall not discuss here the whole of the work of the Spirit in and upon the souls of the saints as they perform all the duties of worship by which they draw near to God through Christ and obtain communion with him. I shall consider it, not in an absolute sense, but only with respect to the aspect under consideration, that is, the extent to which his work renders that worship beautiful and comely.

(i) The Lord Jesus Christ has promised to send his Spirit to believers to enable them, in content and performance, to fulfil every duty required in the word (Isa. 59:21). He will give his word and Spirit. The promise of the one and of the other is of equal extent and breadth. Whatever God presents in his word to be believed, or to be performed, his promise is that he gives his Spirit to enable that belief or performance. There is no promise or precept given for which the Spirit will not enable believers to respond to the mind of God in them; and, conversely, the Spirit is not given in order to fulfil any duty that is not required in the word. The range of the word and of the Spirit, in their separate places, is identical: the one as a moral rule, and the other as a real principle of efficacy. Hence, those who demand duties which are not required in the word will need to look for other aids than those provided by the Spirit of grace; and those who pretend to be led by the Spirit beyond the bounds of the word will need to provide themselves with another gospel. The true gospel abounds with promises such as the following: he shall 'guide us into all truth'; he shall 'teach us all things'; he shall 'abide with us forever.' Having given his disciples precepts for their whole duty to God and to himself, Christ promises his Spirit to them to abide with them and to enable them to accomplish these precepts.

(ii) There are three things necessary for true gospel worship.

Firstly, *light* and *knowledge*, so that we might be acquainted with the mind and will of God with respect to worship; to understand what he accepts and approves, and what it is he appoints, so that we might know 'how to refuse the evil and to choose the good.' We are to be as Christ's sheep, hearing his voice and following him, not listening to the voice of a stranger.

Secondly, *Grace* in the heart, so that in this access to God there may be a true, real, spiritual, saving communion with him, obtained in those acts of faith, love, delight and obedience which he requires. Without this, it is 'impossible to please God' in anything.

Thirdly, the *ability* to perform those duties that God requires in worship in such a way that he may be glorified, and those called to worship edified in their most holy faith.

When these three things concur, there the worship of God is fulfilled in a true manner, according to his own mind and will. Such worship is, consequently, excellent, beautiful and glorious – God himself being judge. These three things believers receive by and from the Spirit of Christ; thus, in this way, they receive from him their access to the Father, that is, they are enabled and supported in the worship which God requires at their hands.

Firstly: *It is the Spirit who helps them discover the mind and will of God concerning worship*, that they may embrace what he has appointed and refuse that of which he will say at the last day, 'Who has required this at your hand?' He is promised to 'guide them into all the truth,' as the Spirit of truth (John 16:13), and is the blessed 'anointing' who teaches them all things (1 John 2:27): all things for the glory of God and for their own consolation. He it is who speaks the words which sound in the ears: 'This is the way, walk in it' (Isa. 30:21). And when Paul prays for the guidance of the saints, he does so by praying that God would give them the 'Spirit of wisdom and revelation' in Christ (Eph. 1:17). The Spirit does this in two ways:

(i) By causing them to listen diligently to the word, Christ's voice, for their direction, and to that alone. This is the great work of the Spirit. We find this in John 16:13, where it is said, 'He will not speak on his own authority, but whatever he hears he will speak'; that is, he will reveal and declare nothing but what is in the mind of Christ, revealed in the word. It is to this that he will call men's attention. His constant call is: 'To the teaching and to the testimony!', that is, 'to the word' (Isa. 8:20). If men turn to any other teaching they remove themselves from the compass of his commission, they depart from that direction which the Father himself first pointed out from heaven: 'This is my beloved Son; hear him.' The Son is the only master and teacher to whom the Spirit carries all believers. He still cries: 'Hear him; attend to him speaking in the word.' It is true that in practice, according to the rule for dealing with scandals and disorders in the church, we are commanded to 'hear the church,' to obey its good directions and to walk according to the gospel, but as to the worship of God, with respect to both the content and rules of its appointments, we are continually called by the Spirit always to hear Christ – and any spirit which sends us to anyone else is not of Christ.

(ii) By revealing the mind of Christ to us in the word. This is his work which he undertakes and performs. I acknowledge that even amongst the saints there are many mistakes in the understanding of the worship of God notwithstanding the assistance that the Spirit is ready to give to them. They are often careless in attending to his directions; negligent in praying for his assistance; superficial in their use of the means appointed by him for the discovery of truths; regardless of clearing their minds of prejudices and temptations that hinder them in the discovery of the mind of God. It is no wonder therefore that they are left to be corrected under their own mistakes and miscarriages. But this does not deny the truth that the Spirit gives the knowledge of the worship of God to believers in the word, because it is not, nor can be, profitably and savingly obtained in any other way. As 'no one can say "Jesus is Lord" except in the Holy Spirit' (1 Cor. 12:3), so no man can know the way of God's house and worship but by the Spirit. We learn from experience that those who despise his assistance prefer to trust to themselves and other men for the worship of God, rather than to the word.

The Spirit fulfils this work, generally, by the use of means. He does it to the extent that, though in some instances there may be mistakes among the saints, yet these are not usually so great as to make their worship unacceptable to God in Christ. And in those things in which, at times, they are 'otherwise minded' than according to the truth, if they continue to wait, these also will be revealed to them from the word by the Spirit. The worship of God cannot be found out by man, but only by the design of him who is 'the wisdom of God.' It is not taught by human wisdom or attainable by human effort, but by the wisdom and revelation of the Spirit of God. In its discovery and growth it is in every way divine and heavenly, as becomes the greatness and holiness of God. For God himself is the only judge of that which pleases him. If anything else sets itself up in competition with it, for beauty and glory, it will find, at the last day, how very unequal the contest.

Secondly: Believers have this access by the Spirit in that *he enables them to approach God spiritually, with grace in their hearts* because he is the Spirit of grace and supplication. This is a specific purpose for which the Spirit is promised to believers, that he might be in them 'a Spirit of grace and pleas for mercy' (Zech. 12:10), enabling them to draw near to God in a gracious and acceptable way. He performs this work when he is bestowed upon them according to the promise (Rom. 8:26, 27). Though men should try their best, they do not know what they should pray for, and it is the Spirit of Christ alone who enables them to fulfil this whole work. If all the men in the world should put their heads together to compose one prayer for the use of one saint for just one day, they would not be able to provide anything that would answer his needs and condition. Nor can any man do it for himself without the help and assistance of the Spirit, whose proper work this is.

It would require a large treatise to show what the Holy Spirit, as a Spirit of grace in the hearts of the believers, performs to this end, so that they, in their access to God, may have a saving, spiritual communion with him in Christ. This is, indeed, the heart of all the glory and beauty that lies in the worship of God. If I were to undertake it, I would have to deal with all the following points:

(i) That the Holy Spirit reveals to them their needs, their state and their condition, together with all the spiritual concerns of their souls. Because of these, no man can come to a saving, spiritual relationship without the effectual working of the Spirit. Many men think that it is an easy thing to know what they want, but he who knows the difficulty of obedience, the deceitfulness of the heart, the wiles of Satan, the tricks and craft of indwelling sin, will not think so, but will acknowledge that this can only be discovered by the Spirit of grace.

(ii) It is he alone who really affects the heart and soul with the sense of their needs, once these are discovered to us. We ourselves are dull and stupid in spiritual things. When matters of the most solemn concern are mentioned, we can pass them by without being affected to any degree comparable to their seriousness and importance. The Holy Spirit deeply affects the heart with its spiritual concerns; works sorrow, fear and desire which are in proportion to the needs discerned; he 'himself intercedes for us with groanings too deep for words.'

(iii) It is he alone who can reveal the saving relief and supplies that God has provided in the promises of the gospel for all the wants of the saints. He therefore enables them to present their requests according to the mind of God. No consideration of the letter of the promises will bring to light savingly the glorious relief provided in them for our needs, but it is revealed to the saints effectually by the Spirit as provided by the love of the Father, purchased by the blood of the Son, and stored up for us in the covenant of grace. We may then make our requests for our share according to the will of God.

(iv) It is the Holy Spirit who works faith, love, delight, zeal, watchfulness, perseverance – all those graces that give the soul communion with God in worship – and renders our prayers effectual in Christ. He does this radically, by creating, conceiving and regenerating them in the hearts of believers, in that first instillation of the new, spiritual, living principle with which they are endued when they are born of him. He does it also as he acts, excites and stirs them up in every duty of the worship of God that the saints are called to. He enables them to act according to the mind of God.

In this way the soul has spiritual communion with God when engaged in the duties of worship, and these topics, together with various other things, are what should be discussed if we aimed to describe the work of the Spirit in gospel worship as he is a Spirit of grace and supplication. But a general mention of them, as above, will be sufficient for my purpose, namely, to present the beauty and glory of that worship that is carried on in such a way. All the beauty of the world fades away before this worship, and becomes as nothing. The glory and excellence belonging to the spiritual communion of the soul in that heavenly intercourse which exists between God and his saints in this worship, brought about by the grace of the Holy Spirit, brings all the outward pomp of ceremonial worship into contempt. The Holy Spirit is essentially God himself, blessed forever in his own name. He comes upon the hearts of the elect and communicates his own grace to them. He then enables them to act, exert and put forth these graces in their worship of God. God delights in them, as coming from himself, as of his own workmanship in us. He sees a return of himself to himself, of his grace to his glory. By these graces, the saints approach into his presence, speak with him, treat with him and hear from him. It is the language of faith and love alone, and kindred graces of his Spirit, that God hears in worship. Other voices, cries and noises, he does not regard. Though some of them, in themselves, might be acceptable to him, yet without the graces of the Spirit, all of them are an abomination to him. Here is the beauty and glory of the worship of the gospel: the beauty and glory that God sees in it. Where it involves the work of the Spirit of God, faith, love, delight and zeal are exercised in a saving and spiritual way. Only an atheist would deny that these are acceptable to God; that this worship is glorious, beautiful and comely. The man who thinks that any outward solemnity can offer worship when these are missing is no better than an atheist. All depends on these spiritual graces.

Thirdly, As from the foundation of the world, so also in the New Testament, the solemn worship of God is to be performed in the assemblies of his saints and people. Wherever this worship is to be offered by many, reason requires that one or more men, according to the need, should stand before that assembly and act as its hand or mouth or eyes. And this is what God has ordained, namely, that in all public assemblies someone should be appointed to lead them in the performing of the duties of worship required by God, whatever these may be. Just as the elements of that worship which these men are to minister before the Lord have been prescribed by God himself, so also he has given these two marks or guides to direct the nature of their ministry: it must be performed in such a way as, firstly, to *glorify* God, and secondly, to *edify* the assembly itself. It would take me too long to show what is involved in this: the practice of public worship to the edification of the congregation. All the ordinances of God must have their proper work and effect in and upon the saints, for the increase of their faith and grace, and for the growth of their obedience and communion with God. The thought of this work made the apostle say, 'Who is sufficient for these things?' (2 Cor. 2:16). Briefly, to the extent that it is possible, their condition is to be spread before the Lord in prayer just as they experience it in their own souls: their desires are to be discerned and expressed; their pleas for mercy and grace to be presented, along with the other functions of prayer. Similarly, the preaching of the word, in its instruction, comfort and exhortation, etc., is to be delivered in a manner that is suited to their condition. The same is true for all other ordinances: they are to be managed and administered in such a way that best tends to the edification of the assembly.

All this is included in the third benefit that the saints receive by the Spirit if they are to approach God. *He gives gifts and abilities: spiritual gifts to those whom he calls to this work of leading the assemblies in the worship of God*, so that they may perform all things to the glory of God and the edification of the body. I shall not even mention the additions that are invented and devised by men for this purpose. Anyone who has known the least communion with God knows also the emptiness and utter insufficiency of these.

There is abundant evidence in the Scriptures that the Holy Spirit furnishes men with gifts for this purpose. Indeed, blessed be God, we have clear evidence of this from those who received such gifts (1 Cor. 12:4, 7, 8, 11). The apostle's purpose in that chapter is to discuss the worship of God as it is to be carried out in the gospel assemblies of the saints, and, as an example, he describes the worship of the church of Corinth. In order that all should be carried out correctly, he begins by stating in the first verse that spiritual gifts are bestowed. He deals first with those gifts provided to enable men to lead the public worship. In the fourth verse he tells us that the author of those gifts is the Holy Spirit: he is sent by Christ for this purpose, to bestow them to the churches. The result of this distribution, he says, is the profit and edification of the whole body (verse 7). Each person who receives gifts does so with this aim: to use them for the good and benefit of the whole. With this end in view, a variety of gifts are bestowed (verse 8), so that by their use the body may be supplied, and the edification of the church continued. Having asserted in this way the nature, purpose and distribution of these gifts, he concludes by again stating that their author is the Holy Spirit (verse 11). Further directions for exercising and using these gifts, built upon this foundation, are provided in various scriptures, such as 1 Peter 4:10, 11.

This work also, then, in the more solemn public worship of God, is fulfilled by that Spirit in whom we have access to the Father. He gives spiritual gifts to men enabling them to perform in a holy, evangelical manner the administering of all ordinances to which they are appointed, so that God may be glorified and the saints edified. He enables men to pray so that the souls of the saints may be drawn forth into communion with God, according to all their wants and desires. He enables men to preach or speak 'as the oracles of God' so that the saints may receive instruction suitable to their conditions, according to the aims of God's good word, whose declaration is committed to them. He enables men to administer the seals of the covenant so that the faith of the saints may be excited and stirred up to act and exert itself according to the nature of each ordinance. And all these gifts are bestowed on men for the good and edification of others. If used in this way they reach further and act more effectively upon the souls of the saints than was ever imagined by him to whom they were entrusted. He little realises how many of his words and expressions, in the infinite wisdom of the Holy Spirit, were exactly suited, in their great variety, to the conditions of the saints. Here, one; there, another, is moved, affected, humbled, melted, lifted up, made to rejoice by them. The Holy Spirit makes them effective to fulfil that for which he gave the gifts from which they flow.

I might mention various other advantages which pertain to our access to God by one Spirit, but because it would be impossible to list all the details, and because they may all be reduced to one or other of these three general points, I shall not mention any more.

This then is the first evidence that we have in this text which reveals the glory, beauty and excellence of gospel worship. In it we have an access to God the Father in the Spirit, in the three aspects which have been described above. There is order found here: The Spirit reveals the mind of God with respect to the worship which is acceptable to him; he provides the souls of the saints with all those graces by which they have communion with God in his worship; he gives gifts to some, enabling them to lead the assemblies in God's worship, according to God's mind, and to their edification. Blessed order – against which the gates of hell shall not prevail! Order, proceeding from the God of order – his own project and appointment! There is beauty, decency and loveliness found here. It is all the work of the glorious and holy Spirit and is, like himself, holy, glorious and beautiful. To set up any human devices in competition with it is that which the Lord's soul abhors.

(2) Just as the saints have access in the gospel to God in the Spirit, so they all have their access *in one Spirit*; and this is the source of that uniformity which God requires. The apostle tells us that, with respect to the gifts, there is a great diversity of them and differences between them (1 Cor. 12:4-6). Where then is the uniformity? One man may have better and greater gifts than another; one man might be the more eminent in a particular gift, another in another; one may excel in prayer, another in prophesying and preaching. What confusion, surely, must result! Where is any uniformity in all this? The apostle answers (verse 11). This is where the uniformity of gospel worship lies, that though the gifts bestowed on men to lead the worship differ, and there is a great diversity among them, yet they are all bestowed by one Spirit, and he does so with that order mentioned above. One and the same Spirit reveals the will and worship of God to them all; one and the same Spirit works the same graces in all their hearts; one and the same Spirit bestows the gifts necessary for leading gospel worship in the public assemblies to those called to that work. What if he is pleased to distribute these gifts to these men in differing particulars: apportioning 'to each one individually as he wills'? This does not hinder the worship in any way, for these saints all approach God by one Spirit. They therefore, throughout the world, exhibit a uniformity. This is true catholic uniformity. Anything going by that name but, in fact, invented by men

will maintain unity only as far as the next hedge, and, as might easily be shown, is the greatest principle of disorder and deformity in the world. But here is the uniformity of gospel worship: all the saints, everywhere, have their access in it to God in one Spirit, who, in general, works in the same way in them all, though he might supply different gifts, providing edification to the whole.

I have discussed these evidences found in the text which prove directly the beauty, excellence, order and uniformity of gospel worship, as considered in and of itself. Before I come to look at its comparative glory, relative to the outward solemn worship of the temple of old, I shall add one further consideration which is necessary in order to answer some objections, as well as to emphasise further the truth being taught: a consideration taken from the place where spiritual worship is performed. Much of the beauty and glory of the old worship, based on carnal ordinances, consisted of the excellence of the place where it was performed: first, Moses' tabernacle, and then the temple of Solomon, whose glory and beauty I shall mention later. Some imagine that there needs to be an equivalent beauty in the place where men gather for gospel worship; accordingly they put much effort into painting and adorning it. But they are wrong, because they do not know the Scriptures. Nothing is said of the place and seat of gospel worship which cannot be understood under three headings; all of which render it glorious:

(i) Gospel worship *is performed in heaven*. Though all who offer it are on earth, yet they do it, by faith, in heaven. The apostle says that believers, in their worship, 'enter the holy places' to which he exhorts them to draw near (Heb. 10:19, 22). What are 'the holy places' to which they enter with their worship? It is where Jesus Christ entered as their forerunner (Heb. 6:20). The phrase refers to heaven itself (Heb. 9:24). You might say, 'How can it be the case that men enter into heaven while they are here below?' I answer, 'Are you "masters in Israel" and yet ask such questions?' Those who have an access to the immediate presence of God, and to the throne of grace, are entering heaven itself. And this adds to the glory which we are considering. What poor, weak thoughts men have of God and his ways if they think there is an acceptable glory and beauty in a little paint and varnish! Heaven itself, the place of God's glorious residence, where he is attended by all his holy angels, that is where this worship takes place. We see the glorious description of it in the whole of Revelation, chapter 4. Though it is only the worship of the church that is described there, it is expressly said to be 'in heaven' (Rev. 4:1). It would be easy to show from the chapter the various aspects of this glory, but I am only touching on the main points.

(ii) *The persons of the saints* who perform this gospel worship *are said to be 'the temple of the Lord'* (1 Cor. 6:19). 'Your body is a temple of the Holy Spirit within you, whom you have from God.' 'Do you not know that you are God's temple ... God's temple is holy, and you are that temple' (1 Cor. 3:16, 17). God does not now have a physical temple, but he has chosen this spiritual one: the hearts and souls of his saints. And these are beautiful temples indeed, being washed with the blood of Christ, made beautiful with the graces of the Spirit, adorned for communion with him. This

why the 'king's daughter' is said to be 'all glorious within'
(Psa. 45:13, KJV; 'All glorious is the princess in her chamber,'
ESV). Whatever men may think, God, who recognises his
own graces in the hearts of his own, and in whose eyes
nothing is beautiful or costly apart from grace, knows and
judges that this place of worship, this temple of his choice,
is full of glory and beauty. Whoever professes to be a Christian, let him be a judge as to which is more beautiful in
God's sight: 'a living stone' adorned with all the graces of
the Spirit, a heart full of the grace of Christ, or a dead stone
cut out of the quarries, even if engraved into the likeness
of a man?

(iii) *The assemblies of the saints are described as God's temple
and as the seat and place of public, solemn gospel worship*
(Eph. 2:21, 22). In these assemblies are found living stones
forming a holy house in the Lord, a dwelling place for God
by the Spirit. God dwells here. Just as he dwelt in the temple
of old, by outward, physical pledges of his presence, so here,
in the assemblies of his saints, which form his habitation,
he dwells in an immeasurably more glorious manner by his
Spirit. Here, according to his promise, is his dwelling place.
The saints' assemblies are now, according to the order of
the gospel, a 'structure … joined together.' Just as the struc-
tures of tabernacle and temple were raised of old, so these
assemblies are raised in their spiritual union in and under
Christ as head. And they are a temple – a holy temple –
holy with 'true holiness,' as the apostle writes (Eph. 4:24);
not a typical or relative holiness, but real holiness, such as
the Lord's soul delights in. I know that some can see no
beauty in the assemblies of the saints unless there is also an

outward beauty and splendour in the fabric and building in which they meet. But what some men can or cannot see is beside the point. Christ himself, for some, 'had no form or majesty that we should look at him.' No more have his saints, his ways or his worship. But this is not what we should look for, but for that which is beautiful, comely and of value in the eyes and judgment of God. Nor are we questioning whether this group, or that, are saints of God or not. The only question is whether or not an assembly of true saints, which are the temple of God, called together in gospel order, form a glorious seat of worship. God says that this is the case. If some men say otherwise, those who are not bewitched by that which I shall not name, will easily know what to believe.[1]

SECONDLY:[2] We next proceed to describe the glory and beauty of gospel worship comparatively; that is, with reference to the solemn outward worship which, by God's appointment, was used in Old Testament times. The latter, as we shall show, was far more excellent with respect to outward splendour and beauty, on many accounts, than anything of a similar nature devised by men. I am all the more willing to do this because the Holy Spirit so often and so frequently insists upon it in the New Testament,

[1] This sermon was printed posthumously in 1721 but would have been preached sometime between 1673 and 1683. Owen, presumably, is here referring indirectly to innovations that were being reintroduced progressively at that time in the national church as a result of the restoration of Episcopacy and of the High Church system of William Laud.

[2] According to the two main divisions for these two sermons, as given on p. 96 above.—G.

with many great and weighty reasons, and had suggested it beforehand in many places in the Old Testament. In order to arrive at a proper understanding of what is gospel, and what is revealed in Scripture on this account, some things need to be considered beforehand.

(i) As the whole worship of the old church was by God's own appointment, so also were all its rites, ceremonies and ornaments, both in the tabernacle and in the temple.

Without exception, every part of the fabric of the worship and every ornament involved – every rite and cere-mony that attended it – was wholly of God's design and command. This is known and acknowledged. Moses made all things 'according to the pattern that was shown' him on the mountain. When he had finished the whole work, it is repeated eight times in one chapter (Exod. 40) that he had done as the Lord had commanded him. Surely this gave the worship a beauty, order and glory greater than anything the wisest of men could invent. 'Woe to him who strives with him who made him, a pot among earthen pots!' (Isa. 45:9). The worship of the pope and his inventions may possibly outdo the beauty and order of the worship of the Turk and his inventions, but I hope they will not compare themselves with God, nor make themselves equal to him. But why say I hope it, when the opposite is clear for all to see? Does he not undertake to prescribe rules of his own in the worship of God? By doing so, doesn't he make himself equal with God, whose prerogative it is to be the only lawgiver to his people's conscience and the only prescriber of his own worship? But I may still hope for one thing, namely, that men will not blatantly argue that what is of their appointment is equal to

and comparable to that which God appoints. If their institutions and God's are compared together, the former will
surely be found at a great disadvantage. This, I hope, will be
generally acknowledged, yet men are very prone in practice
to make void the commands of God by their traditions and
institutions, laying more weight on some of them than on
all the commands of Jesus Christ.

Some might argue: 'But it may be that when God
appointed the worship of old, together with all its details,
he did not intend that it should be beautiful and glorious,
but plain and homely. It does not therefore follow that it
is beautiful and excellent merely because he appointed it.'
Answer: Though we may safely trust in the general proposition that what God has appointed for his own worship
is necessarily beautiful, glorious, excellent, orderly and
comely, specifically because it is of his appointment, yet I
might add:

(ii) That it was God's intention to appoint and dispose of
all the details specifically in order that the solemnity of his
worship might be very beautiful and glorious.

He appoints the high priest's garments to be made
expressly 'for glory and for beauty' (Exod. 28:2): attractive
and pleasant to the eye. When he speaks of the institution
of the church, formed and fashioned by himself, he says
that its renown went forth among the heathen for its beauty,
in that it was perfect through the splendour that he had
bestowed upon it (Ezek. 16:14). A renowned beauty and a
perfect comeliness belonged to its ways of worship, so that
the prophet declares: 'a glorious throne set on high from
the beginning is the place of our sanctuary' (Jer. 17:12). But

I do not need to multiply testimonies. Everyone knows what is said everywhere in the Scriptures of the tabernacle, the temple, and all the worship associated with them. As God appointed, so it came to pass: it was the most beautiful solemnity that ever the sun shone upon. Mosaic worship, as celebrated in Solomon's temple, outdid all the glory and splendour that was ever enjoyed, in any place or age from the beginning of the world. If all the princes of Egypt had gathered up all their wealth they would not have been able to build a fabric of such cost, magnificence and glory as Solomon's temple. To list the details would be endless. The garments of the high priest presented him as a figure of such awe and glory that Alexander the Great, that famous conqueror of the east, would have fallen down before him, prostrate with reverence. The order of the house and all the worship in it: who could consider it without admiration? How glorious was Solomon's house when it stood in its greatest order and beauty, all overlaid with gold, with thousands of priests and Levites ministering in their orders, with their most solemn musical instruments, and the great assembled congregation of hundreds of thousands, all singing praises to God! If any man gives a little thought to compare the greatest, most solemn pomp and costly worship invented by any of the sons of men and introduced into the Christian church in these latter days, with this religion of Israel, he will quickly find that there is no comparison. It is all a toy, an empty thing, in comparison. Take the cathedral of Peter in Rome; bring in the pope and all his cardinals in all their vestments, accessories and ornaments; fill the choir with the best singers they can get; set out and decorate their images and pictures to the utmost that their treasures and superstitions can supply: then compare it to Solomon's temple and its worship, and – without even considering that the one was from heaven, and the other is of men – the very nature of the elements involved would reveal how vain are the pretences to glory and beauty. And how much more is this the case for those more subordinate pretenders that may be found!

These things being understood, I now state that, even though this whole worship and all its concerns were appointed by God himself; even though it was the very pinnacle of that which external beauty and splendour could reach, yet it was not in any way comparable to the beauty and glory of this spiritual worship of the New Testament; indeed, it had no glory in comparison with it. I shall briefly demonstrate this: (a) in general; and then, (b) by arguing from particular instances.

(a) For the general case, I need go no further than the apostle's argument where he deals explicitly with this comparison, namely, 2 Corinthians 3:7-10. He here deliberately compares the ministry of the law in the letter, with all its outward legal worship, rites and ceremonies, with the administration of the gospel in the Spirit, and its attendant worship of God. He first acknowledges that the old administration was very glorious, by either providing an instance of it, or proving it, by the example of the shining of Moses' face when he came down from the mount, after he had received the law and the pattern of all the worship which he was to appoint for that church. It seems that God left that shining on Moses' face – so strong that the people could not bear its brightness – to testify to the glory of that which had now been revealed to him. Indeed, therefore, says the apostle, 'That ministration was glorious, very glorious – truly, glory in the abstract' (verse 9). There had been nothing in the world to compare with it. Let us now, then, compare it with the ministration of the Spirit and the worship of God under the gospel. Perhaps the apostle, in this case, will say: 'Indeed, it is not quite so glorious.' But no, he goes further, and tells us that the latter so far exceeds it in glory, comeliness and excellence that, in comparison, the other had no glory at all! What then may be said of the glory and beauty of anything invented by men in the worship of God? I do not dare say what the apostle says of that which God himself appointed: that it has any glory and beauty in itself. But suppose that it had. Let men esteem it as glorious and beautiful as they can possibly fancy it to be; yet – unless the same veil is on their minds when reading the gospel as that which is on the Jews when reading Moses – they will have to see and acknowledge that it has no glory compared to that spiritual worship which I have just described.

(b) Some particular examples will make the general comparison clearer. I will list only three of these, which, in that they were the main springs of all the beauty, glory and order of the old worship, are specifically mentioned by the apostle in this respect in the Epistle to the Hebrews. There he demonstrates that the excellence of the evangelical administrations of the covenant and worship of God are above and beyond the old legal situation.

(i) The first of these was the temple, the seat of all the solemn outward worship of the old church. I have mentioned its beauty previously and shall not repeat any particular

description of it. It is sufficient that it was the most important site of the beauty and order of Judaic worship, and it
rendered all that worship glorious, to such an extent that
the people idolized it and put their trust in it; believing that
because of it they should certainly be preserved notwithstanding their presumptuous sins. Indeed, it had such
blessings and promises annexed to it that if there were
today any such house or place in the world like it, I would
wish to be one of the first to embark on a pilgrimage to
it, though it were twice as far away as Jerusalem. Yet, in
spite of all this, when Solomon himself prays at the dedication of that house (1 Kings 8:27), he seems to suggest that
there was a limit to his praise with respect to the degree
to which the temple answered to the great majesty of God.
It was a house on the earth; a house that he built with his
own hands. This suggests that he looked beyond to a more
glorious house than that. And what would that temple be, if
it were compared with the temple of gospel worship? That
which is now called the temple of the people of God is as
much beyond that of old as spiritual things are beyond the
physical, as heavenly is beyond earthly, as eternal is beyond
temporal.

In the first place, the body of Christ himself is our temple,
in one sense, as he himself referred to it when speaking of
the temple of his body as being prefigured by Jerusalem's
temple. He has the fullness of the Godhead dwelling in him,
as was typified by the presence of God in the old temple, and
he is the centre where all his people meet with their worship
of God, as did those of old in the temple. And surely there
is no comparison, for beauty and excellence, between the
house that Solomon built and the Son of God, 'who is the

radiance of the glory of God and the exact imprint of his nature.'

Again, the persons and assemblies of the saints are a temple to God, under the gospel, as I mentioned before. They are his body (Eph. 1:23) and his house (Heb. 3:6). Nor is the old temple, made of wood and stones, gold and silver, to be compared with this living house, washed with the blood of Christ, adorned with the real graces of the Spirit and garnished with all the choice jewels of God's eternal love. They are God's delight, the 'first-fruits of his creatures' to him (James 1:18); the spouse of Christ – altogether lovely through his graces. The Lord Jesus sees more beauty and glory in the weakest assembly of his saints, coming together, acted upon and guided in his worship and ways by his Spirit, than was ever in all the worship of Solomon's temple when it was in its glory.

Thirdly, heaven itself, the holy place not made with hands, is also the saints' temple under the gospel. Believers have in their worship an open way into the holiest, made for them by Christ who entered into it as the forerunner (Heb. 6:20), opening it for them and also giving admission into it (Heb. 10:19-21). How greatly does this exalt the excellence of the spiritual worship of the gospel! What was the glory of Solomon's temple compared to the glory of the meanest star in heaven? How much less was it in comparison with the glorious presence of God in the highest heavens, where believers enter with all their worship, even where Christ sits at the right hand of God?

(ii) The second spring of the beauty of the old worship – indeed, it was the hinge upon which it all turned – was the priesthood of Aaron, together with all the administrations committed to his charge. The pomp, state and ceremonies that the Papists have invented in their outward worship, or that heap which, in several parcels, they have borrowed from the heathen and the Jews, are mere toys in comparison with the magnificence of the Aaronic administrations. But the high priest under the gospel is Christ alone. I need not take pains to compare these with one another; partly because it is confessed by all that Christ is incomparably more excellent and glorious, and partly because the apostle, for this very purpose, develops this comparison in various instances in the Epistle to the Hebrews. All may find it and read it there, in that it is the main subject of that most excellent epistle.

(iii) The order, glory, number and significance of their sacrifices was another part of their glory. Indeed, anyone who contemplates seriously that one solemn anniversary sacrifice of expiation and atonement instituted in chapter 16 of Leviticus will quickly see that there was great glory and solemnity in its outward ceremony. 'But now,' says the apostle, 'we have "a better sacrifice" than these' (Heb. 9:23). We have him who is the high priest, the altar, and the sacrifice – all himself. His worth, value, glory and beauty – on the basis of his own person, the efficacy of his oblation and its true effect – is more than the whole creation, if it were possible to have offered it up as one sacrifice. This is the standing sacrifice for the saints, offered 'once for all,' as effective at any time as if it had been offered daily. Of any other sacrifices, properly so called, the saints have none.

I might mention other particulars, but I think that, through the grace of the Lord Jesus Christ, I have, in some measure, manifested the excellence, beauty, order and uni-formity of the spiritual worship of the gospel. I have done so both absolutely in itself, and in comparison with any other way of worship whatsoever. From all this, it may easily be seen that our gospel worship may certainly be considered as among the inexpressible privileges purchased for us by the death of Christ, as I first observed at the commence-ment of these sermons.[3]

[3] See p. 94.

Sermon 8

The Beauty and Strength of Zion[1]

Walk about Zion, go round her, number her towers, consider well her ramparts, go through her citadels, that you may tell the next generation that this is God, our God for ever and ever. He will guide us for ever.—Psa. 48:12-14

MANY commentators think that this psalm is an 'ἐπινίχιον': a triumphant song of thanksgiving, after some great deliverance at Jerusalem. Some apply it to King Asa's time, when Zerah and the Ethiopians came with an army of a million men against Jerusalem. Others refer it to the times of Jehosaphat when the Moabites, the Ammonites, and Mount Seir (the Edomites) were gathered together against Judah; others, again, to the days of Hezekiah, when Sennacherib and his army came against Jerusalem and were destroyed.[2] They base their interpretation on verses 4 to 6: 'For behold, the kings assembled; they came on together. As soon as they saw it, they were astounded; they were in panic; they took to flight. Trembling took hold of them there, anguish as of a woman in labour.' This is a description of some great

---

[1] Preached on 19 April, 1675.—G.
[2] See 2 Chron. 14:9-15; 2 Chron. 20:1-30; 2 Kings, chapters 18 and 19, respectively.

consternation that fell upon God's enemies, and Jerusalem's enemies, as they drew near to Jerusalem. This also is how the Jews interpret these verses. 'Walk about Zion, go round her, number her towers, consider well her ramparts, go through her citadels,' that is, notwithstanding this great attack, whether by Ethiopians, Moabites or Sennacherib, not one tower of Zion or Jerusalem has been brought down; all things are safe and well. For my own part, I would judge, rather, that this psalm was composed by David, and is therefore purely prophetic and spiritual. It is easy to show that all the psalms leading up to Psalm 48 are so. The close of the previous psalm speaks of the calling of the Gentiles, where he says, 'God reigns over the nations; God sits on his holy throne' (verse 8). And in verse 9, we have the marginal reading, which is better than the text: 'The voluntary of the people are gathered unto the people of the God of Abraham' (Psa. 47:9; KJV, margin). The people had become a willing people in the day of his power. However, all agree that these words are a graphic description, set before us by the psalmist, of the defence that God will provide for his church at all times.

Notice how carefully he requires us to view the scene that he is considering. He sees Zion as a well-fortified garrison, not likely to be taken quickly by an enemy. He calls on us to pay particular attention to the fortifications, providing the appropriate directions to ensure that we see everything: '"Walk about Zion," this is how you will see how well she is defended. Perhaps you have walked some distance and observed much, but do not stop. "Go round her." Are there any weak spots where she might be attacked by the enemy? "Number her towers," see how many there are of them.' This is what a man of judgment and understanding would do if he were to survey a defended position and judge whether it would hold out against a strong attack. '"Consider well her ramparts." Do not take just a general view of Zion's defences but evaluate them carefully; decide whether they are likely to hold out or not, and whether you can put your trust in them. "Go through her citadels."' These last were the great buildings in and around Zion, called in some places 'ivory palaces' because of their decoration. We have here, therefore, directions given for a careful, detailed and discerning survey of the fortifications of Zion, since it will certainly be attacked by great and powerful enemies. Two other things are added: firstly, the specific reason why this should be done, 'That you may tell the next generation.' Other ages of the church need to possess the knowledge of these defences. And secondly, why this would be of benefit to them and to the generations that followed them – 'This is God, our God for ever and ever. He will guide us for ever.'

I shall draw only one point from these words and speak very briefly and plainly on it:

Observation: A diligent search into, and a consideration of, the means and causes of the preservation and protection of the church in its greatest dangers and difficulties, is a duty that is required of us, for our own support against sinful fears and also to enable us to bear that testimony needed by future generations to encourage them to trust in the Lord.

Every age should present a good testimony to the next generation of the Lord's dealings with Zion. It is a duty laid upon us to search and enquire diligently into the causes and means of the protection and preservation of God's church, in the midst of imminent dangers and difficulties, so that we may be strengthened against sinful fears in ourselves and encourage those after us to trust in the Lord. Just as we have received such a testimony from those who went before us, so we are to do the same to those who shall follow us.

All that I shall do, presently, is to answer these five questions:

1. What are we to understand by the preservation and protection of the church? This needs to be known so that we do not look for less than, or more than, that which we are likely to encounter.

2. What is meant by searching into, and considering, these causes and means of the church's preservation? 'Walk about Zion, go round her, number her towers, consider well her ramparts, go through her citadels, etc.'

3. What are those causes and means that preserve the church, those towers and ramparts that will not fail whenever Zerah or Sennacherib comes, or whatever attempts are made against Zion?

4. What is the reason why we should search in this way, and look into these causes of the church's protection?

5. What testimony do we have to give with regard to this matter to the next generation? 'That you may tell the next generation.'

Question 1. *What is that preservation and protection of Zion, the church of God, which we should expect, whose causes and means we are to investigate?*

This may be reduced to three points.

(a) *The eternal salvation of the church of God.* This is the goal and the prize which drives all this great running about in the world. Satan, in his own nature, is as active and restless as he is malicious. Yet if this was removed, if this was not always before his eyes (namely, the eternal salvation of the church, of all that believe), I imagine he would give himself much more leisure than he does. All that we experience here: evils, trials, persecutions and so on, are only skirmishes, but if eternal bliss were to be lost, that would be his victory. This, therefore, is part of that preservation and safety of Zion that we are to consider, namely, that 'all Israel will be saved,' as the apostle tells us (Rom. 11:26). The great certainty of this was guaranteed by our Lord Jesus Christ himself: 'My sheep hear my voice, and I know them, and they follow me. I give them eternal life, and they will never perish, and no one will snatch them out of my hand...I and the Father are one' (John 10:27).

This is the first point with respect to the church's preservation, that however great, however severe the conflict, all true believers will be saved eternally. If we do not maintain this thought constantly in our minds, all our concerns over other things will be of no help to us. One false opinion does more mischief to the honour of God in the world, in this respect, than all that the devils are able to do, namely, the belief in the possibility of the total and final apostasy of true believers. For if this were the case, we would have lost the very first principle of the preservation of Zion: the truth that 'all Israel will be saved,' that no one can snatch believers out of Christ's hands.

(b) The truth that *there will be a church, a professing church, kept in the world throughout all generations, despite all the opposition of Satan and the world*. That is, there will be a chosen people, yielding obedience inwardly to Christ and openly professing that obedience, who will be preserved at all times, until the end of the world. This is expressly included in that promise: 'Of the increase of his government and of peace there will be no end, on the throne of David and over his kingdom, to establish it and to uphold it with justice and with righteousness from this time forth and for evermore. The zeal of the Lord of hosts will do this' (Isa. 9:7). Whatever may occur in various places and nations, yet Zion will be preserved. God will reserve a church for Jesus Christ that will visibly profess and yield obedience to him according to the gospel.

But you will say, perhaps, 'Where was such a church at the time of the Antichristian apostasy? Didn't the visible church fail entirely at that time?'

I would answer: Though I acknowledge that all the churches in the world have greatly apostatized and fallen away, yet, firstly, all did not fall away to the same degree as the churches of those countries under the dominion of the Antichristian apostasy. There were churches in the east which, though very corrupt formerly, and even more so now, yet might still justly be considered a visible church. The church of God at the time was in Babylon up until the Reformation. There were, still, in the Roman church a number of people who sincerely feared God and belonged to the Zion of Christ, who were preserved. To them went out that call, 'Come out of her, my people' (Rev. 18:4). Christ's people were in her until the time came that God gave them a call to come out of her. Other groups of them remained in continual visible opposition to the growing apostasy of the papacy. About four or five hundred years after Christ the great amalgamation was made between Christianity and paganism, when the outer court was given up to be trodden down by the Gentiles; that is, when those northern tribes who divided and destroyed the Roman empire were accepted as Christians. Upon that amalgamation, nations professed Christianity and yielded obedience to Christian rulers – bishops, priests and the like – but kept their pagan worship and behaviour. But from that time, when all things sunk into Antichristianism, there was still a visible testimony given against it by the church of Christ, that is, by believers from one generation to another: an eminent, blessed testimony against all that cursed apostasy.

It is good to keep our faith and expectation within bounds; that is, we are not to look for more than is likely to happen, yet we must still be confirmed in our faith in those things that will surely not fail. 'All Israel will be saved,' and Christ will maintain his kingdom. The cause in which we are engaged will be triumphant whatever happens to us. Believers will be saved and a professing church will be preserved, and this is the cause which we serve. And it may well be that God has placed us, in this age, to deliver a specific testimony to a future generation.

(c) Also involved in this image of fortifications is the preservation of the true church of God *by its protection and deliverance from persecution*. We are prone to be more concerned with our own problems and imagine that this third point is more relevant for us than the first two. But this is to make a wrong judgment, for the focus of all our concerns for present deliverance or for the conflicts of the church must be upon the two general goals: the eternal salvation of the church at last, and the preservation of the kingdom of Christ in the world. If we once begin to measure these in terms of our own advantages, peace, liberty and relationships, we shall come to wrong conclusions with respect to God's providence and to our own expectations.

There are three seasons, or three ways, by which churches are in particular danger of coming short of this protection, or to seem to do so: (i) When the power of Satan and of the world are engaged in their persecution. (ii) When the nations of the world among whom they live are so wicked that God will not hold back a general devastation and destruction. (iii) When they themselves apostatize and decay, and provoke God to remove his candlestick from among them.

At such periods it is a matter of trial whether particular churches, or a church in a particular place, will be preserved and protected or not. I confess to you that I believe that all three circumstances are true of us presently, which makes our case so difficult and hard to determine. Yet, I bless God, I think that what we fear most is the least to be feared. It is clear that we fear the first possibility most of all, and I am quite certain that that is the least to be feared. I will mention each of them briefly.

(i) There are two rules by which to judge the state of the church at a time of persecution. One is given by the prophet Hosea: 'Ephraim compasseth me about with lies, and the house of Israel with deceit: but Judah yet ruleth with God, and is faithful with the saints'³ (Hosea 11:12, KJV). He is

---

³ Owen draws his argument from this KJV rendering of verse 12; the ESV reads, 'Ephraim has surrounded me with lies, and the house of Israel with deceit, but Judah still walks with God and is faithful to the Holy One.'

prophesying of the immediate destruction of Ephraim: the church of Israel will wander to Assyria (verse 5), but Judah will remain. Why? 'Judah yet ruleth with God'; that is, 'for God': the ruling power of Judah is for God. I take that to be the meaning of the words, for it was the case with Judah that anything good among them was to be found in the ruling power. Even in the days of Josiah, Judah, that is, the body of the people, turned to God insincerely, and not with their whole heart (Jer. 3:10). But the prophet foresees a time when Judah will not be so. He will rule, therefore, while he is faithful with God. This then is the first rule: While the governing power of a church or nation is for God, is faithful to God and his interest, walking with him, they are within the ramparts. And if I was to say what I truly believe (though in everything that lies in the future for which we do not have clear and full evidence, we must allow for God's sovereignty), wherever churches are found walking with God, ruling for God and faithful to him, they will never in any place be overcome by outward persecution. The only exception might be if this were necessary, in the hidden design of sovereign wisdom, so as to remove gospel witness from a particular place. This case would be an example of the second rule, which is that we can never know, and are left in the dark, as to whether any particular church in this or that place will be absolutely preserved. If God pleases, he can make a general scattering be the means of spreading the gospel. But to the extent that they walk with God they remain within this protection.

(ii) A danger to a church may arise if it found at a place which is to be visited by destruction because of national sins. There were in the days of Jehoiakim and Zedekiah 'good figs, like first-ripe figs,' that is, there were many precious saints of God in the land, but there were also 'very bad figs, so bad that they could not be eaten.' Yet, God put all these figs into a basket, good and bad, for all to go into captivity (Jer. 24:1-10). He could no longer restrain his anger towards the provoking sins of the nation; the whole must go into captivity together. Now if such a time should befall a land, as has occurred, deservedly, to many nations because of national sins, the good may suffer with the bad and churches may be scattered.

(iii) The third danger is their own apostasy. There is nothing in the world that we should fear more than the scattering of a church because of its apostatizing condition. For then we would be bearing the burden of our own guilt as we are scattered, and would lose all hope of retrieving it.

But all churches walking with God are included within the preservation and protection promised in this text, and described as being round about Zion. It is an act of pure sovereignty when God deals differently with any.

Question 2. *What is meant by searching into, and evaluating the causes and means of the church's preservation?* Where should we be looking for this?

(a) First, take your eyes away from those things which will never prove to be ramparts for Zion. You know how such things were blamed in the account given in Isaiah, chapter 22, at a time of great distress and invasion. The prophet tells us what the people did: 'He has taken away the covering of Judah. In that day you looked to the weapons of the House of the Forest, and you saw that the breaches of the city of David were many. You collected the waters of the lower pool, and you counted the houses of Jerusalem, and you broke down the houses to fortify the wall. You made a reservoir between the two walls for the water of the old pool. But you did not look to him who did it, or see him who planned it long ago' (verses 8-11). Looking to carnal help and assistance on our problems and difficulties has been our folly. The first thing in this call to search out Zion is to 'stop regarding man in whose nostrils is breath, for of what account is he?' (Isa. 2:22).

(b) Where shall we look for these ramparts? We must look for the protection of the church in the same place as we look for the destruction of her enemies. And where would that be? The prophet tells us: 'Seek and read from the book of the Lord: Not one of these shall be missing; none shall be without her mate. For the mouth of the Lord has commanded, and his Spirit has gathered them' (Isa. 34:16). The previous prophecy had related to the utter destruction of Edom in type (verses 5, 9), but in antitype it referred to Babylon, Rome, Antichrist. And the verses from 11 to 15 describe the gathering of all the birds of prey, birds of doom, to possess the land. But how do we know whether this will happen? The prophet says, 'Seek out God's book and read; none of these things will fail'; that is, not one specific judgment that God has threatened in the whole of his book against his adversaries shall ever fail. Not in any circumstance: not one hawk or night bird shall be without its mate. Search it out in the book of the Lord, you will find it recorded in these prophecies. And nothing will fail there, for the mouth of the Lord has spoken it, and the Spirit of the Lord will fulfil it.

[155]

We are to look, therefore, and search in the book of the Lord for these defences, causes, and means for the protection of Zion. This is 'the tower of David' where 'hang a thousand shields, all of them shields of warriors' (Song of Sol. 4:4), where all the defence of the church and people of God is recorded. It is your duty to search in God's book, and read to see the means of protecting and preserving the church, and when you have discovered them you are to think deeply about them. Want of consideration greatly weakens our faith. If you can find, by reading God's book, that there are such and such defences and ramparts to Zion, our duty then is to judge whether they will hold out against the greatest attacks and attempts of Satan and all our enemies. I am speaking plainly and with great relevance for today. When you discover these defences, bring them to the shield of faith and to obedience to God and decide whether they are likely to hold out. Consider and judge each one individually. If you are satisfied, trust yourself to them. Gather all that you have, all your concerns, into the compass of these fortifications and trust to them.

This should be a sufficient answer to the second question: Where are we to look for the preservation and protection of the church?

Question 3. *What are those causes and means that preserve Zion and protect the church?*

I can only point out a few aspects of the text. I cannot walk about Zion, I cannot number her towers, but I can consider some of her ramparts that will prove a sure preservation against all opposition. I will note four or five:

(a) *The designation and appointment of Jesus Christ as king of the church, king of Zion*, is the great bulwark of Zion. This is the royal fort that never fails. 'Why do the nations rage and the peoples plot in vain? The kings of the earth set themselves, and the rulers take counsel together, against the Lord and against his anointed, saying, "Let us burst their bonds apart and cast away their cords from us." He who sits in the heavens laughs; the Lord holds them in derision. Then he will speak to them in his wrath, and terrify them in his fury, saying, "As for me, I have set my King on Zion, my holy hill"' (Psa. 2:1-6). 'Regardless of all this tumult, conspiracy and rage, all this counselling and advising,' says the Lord, 'yet, Zion must stand; for I have set my king; I have anointed Christ, my eternal Son, to be king upon my holy hill of Zion.' Yet although Christ has been made king, it does not follow that he might not resign his throne, and thus cease to secure it. Indeed, the truth is that he *will* do so: he will bring his mediatorial reign over his kingdom to an end.[4] But not before he has defeated all his enemies: 'Sit at my right hand, until I make your enemies your footstool' (Psa. 110:1). And the apostle tells us: 'He must reign until he has put all his enemies under his feet' (1 Cor. 15:25). Only when he has defeated all power and authority will he give up the kingdom. This is the source of the great security of the church: that Christ has been made king of Zion. And if

[4] Owen gives a detailed description of the continuation of Christ's mediatorial office in heaven in the last chapter of his treatise on 'The Person of Christ' (*Works*, Vol. 1, London: Banner of Truth Trust, 1965), pp. 252-272. The treatise was originally published four years after this sermon was delivered.—W. H. Goold.

he is a king, he must have subjects. The word is his law; he rules by his Spirit. But rule and law together will not make a kingdom unless there are subjects to yield obedience. If Christ is a king, if he sits over Zion, then the church must be preserved: for he must have a kingdom. There is only one action of the world that will bring about an end to Christ's reign, and that is to stop being his enemy. For the designated period of his reign is: 'Until he has put all his enemies under his feet.' How easy it would be for me to expand on this: that the king of the church has the power to preserve it to all ages and in all circumstances. He has power to keep it for eternal salvation, whether in a visible profession or in particular trials! And what king is there among men who will not save his subjects when they are tried, if it is in his power to do so? The Lord Christ will preserve them: 'I give them eternal life … and no one will snatch them out of my hand' (John 10:28). He is able to save to the uttermost those who draw near to God through him, and he is given to be head over all things to the church: to dispose of all things as seems best to him, for the purpose, the use and the benefit of the church.

This is the first rampart and security that we have to preserve and protect the church, and unless men can dethrone Jesus Christ and throw him down from being king upon the holy hill of Zion, it is in vain for any to think of prevailing against the church.

(b) The second rampart of Zion lies in *the promises of God* which are innumerable. I will only name two of them. One is the foundation of the Old Testament, and the other is the foundation of the New. One held out for four thousand years and was never set aside, and the other has continued for these last sixteen hundred years and will never be shaken.

The promise that was the foundation of the Old Testament was the first promise of God, 'I will put enmity between you and the woman, and between your offspring and her offspring; he shall bruise your head, and you shall bruise his heel' (Gen. 3:15). There are four things in this promise:

(i) That there will always be a two-fold seed in the world: the seed, or offspring, of the serpent, and the offspring of the woman. These shall remain while the world stands.

(ii) That these two seeds will always be at enmity: there will be continual conflict, from the entrance of sin until its end. 'I will put enmity,' says God, and the nature of the enmity is such that it is conducted by means of the highest and most severe warfare. The enmity is spiritual but the warfare is often physical. The first manifestation of this warfare was in blood. Cain killed Abel. Why? Because Cain was of the evil one. In this way the enmity has been carried on in blood from that day to this.

(iii) Each seed has a leader: there is a 'he' and a 'you'; that is, Christ and Satan. Christ is the leader of the seed of the woman, its captain and head in this great conflict; Satan, just as he was the head of the apostasy from God, continues as the head of his seed, the generation of vipers, maintaining the contest with Christ until the end.

(iv) The victory will always be to the offspring of the woman. It is indeed said, 'You shall bruise his heel': Christ's heel, bruised in his sufferings, both in his own person and those of the church. But it is also said, 'He will bruise your head': break your power and strength; conquer you. Zion is therefore safe. This was the foundation of the Old Testament, and although the people were often brought to great distress, sometimes by apostasy and sometimes by persecution, yet this promise carried them and delivered the church safely into the hands of Christ.

And when Christ took the church and proceeded to form it anew, to fashion it to the greater glory of God, he provided the foundation-promise of the New Testament: 'On this rock I will build my church, and the gates of hell shall not prevail against it' (Matt. 16:18). If that more obscure promise under the Old Testament kept Zion secure against all the enmity described for four thousand years, should we not trust to this promise of the Saviour for half that time? Though, in fact, it is the continuance of the same promise, for the 'gates of hell' is the offspring of the serpent, and the 'rock' is Christ.

This is the second rampart of Zion. We may be shaken in our faith and confidence, but we have the promise of God which has supported us thus far in the world and will certainly preserve us to the end.

(c) Thirdly, there is *the watchful providence of God over the church*. This is described in Deuteronomy 11:12, where the land is said to be 'a land that the Lord your God cares for. The eyes of the Lord your God are always upon it, from the beginning of the year to the end of the year.' God cares for the land which is in the church's possession, the seat of God's worship: that is, the church itself. It is described similarly in

Isaiah 27:2, 3, where it is called God's vineyard. 'I, the Lord, am its keeper; every moment I water it. Lest anyone punish it, I keep it night and day.' Here is the watchful providence of God over the church, preserving it night and day. On this providence we live, though it is secret and invisible to us. There is power in it, but 'God hides his power.' We see little, and fail to discern anything to any great extent, of the secret issuing of divine power and wisdom in the hearts and counsels of all mankind. God's purpose in it is to preserve his church, governing the affections of men, ruling their thoughts, turning and overturning their counsels. These providences, in all their circumstances and purposes, will never come to light until the great day when the thoughts of all hearts will be discovered. The Lord will keep and protect his church so that none may hurt it.

(d) Another rampart is *God's secret presence*. God is particularly present in his church. I have written of the nature and special presence of God and Christ in the church, and proved it from many promises, showing its effect, and so will not deal with it now, but only emphasize that it is one of the bulwarks of the church. In Isaiah 8:9, 10 there is a challenge thrown out to all the enemies of God, a challenge to do their worst: 'Be broken, you peoples, and be shattered; give ear, all you far countries; strap on your armour and be shattered. Take counsel together, but it will come to nothing; speak a word, but it will not stand.' What is the reason for this? 'For God is with us.' The presence of God is with his church. Every force, counsel, association or agreement: everything will be broken and come to nothing; it will have no effect. And the only reason he gives is, 'Because

God is with us.' While God is with his church it may be exercised by great trials, so that they might think that they have lost his presence, as in Judges 6:12, 'The angel of the Lord appeared to [Gideon] and said to him, "The Lord is with you, O mighty man of valour." He answered, "If the Lord is with us, why then has all this happened to us?" Why has all this evil come upon us, that we should be under the power of the Midianites, oppressed and destroyed by them?' He could not believe that they could be so oppressed and destroyed by their enemies, if God was with them. Great troubles may fall upon God's church while God is present with them, so that, at times, they are ready to say: 'My way is hidden from the Lord, and my right is disregarded by my God. The Lord has forsaken me; my Lord has forgotten me' (Isa. 40:27; 49:14). 'It cannot be that God is with us,' said Gideon, 'when we are so ruined.' But he will appear and show himself and protect Zion.

(e) The last rampart, which encompasses all these others, is *God's covenant*. 'For this God is our God.' That God who fortified Zion in all other generations and brought about all these deliverances, he is our God in covenant.

I do not need to list any more than these five ramparts of the church. Consider and ponder whether or not they are likely to be sufficient for the preservation of the church. And if God gives us wisdom to single out these things, and view them correctly, we shall soon see what encouragement we have to pray for the protection of the church, whatever may be the attacks on it, even in our days.

Question 4. *What reason is there why we should search in this way, and look into these causes of the church's protection?*

The reason for all this is so that we might free ourselves from our sinful fears and do so by discovering the great mistake made by all our enemies. The reason, the foundation, of all their attacks upon the church is no other than that given in Ezekiel 38:10, 11, 'Thus says the Lord God: On that day, thoughts will come into your mind, and you will devise an evil scheme and say, "I will go up against the land of the unwalled villages. I will fall upon the quiet people who dwell securely, all of them dwelling without walls, and having no bars or gates."' Here is the basis of the assaults of the world against the church in every age: that they have no defences, that they are a poor people that dwell in unwalled villages, having no bars or gates. It is a miserable disappointment for men to determine to destroy or oppress some place, thinking that it is unprotected, and then to find, when they arrive, that things are very different. It is the case today that no one would say a word against the people of God except for this reason: they think they have no defence or protection. And sometimes they proceed with their assault to such an extent that they begin to discover the ramparts of Zion, or at least their effects, if not their causes. The old world did not see God as the cause of his actions, but when the waters began to rise, the psalmist tells us: 'They saw you and were afraid' (Psa. 77:16). 'Is this the people that dwell in unwalled villages that have no bars or gates? Look at their towers! Behold their ramparts! We cannot attack them!' Once God makes them see that Christ's power is engaged for his people, they will cry to the mountains and to the rocks to hide them from the day of his wrath; they will be surprised by fear.

In that the enemies of Christ's church are certainly mistaken presently in their attacks on the church, because, as they imagine, it has no defences (though they will find out at last that there is a defence, which they had not seen or known of), why should we be afraid? There is nothing more encouraging than when one knows that one's enemies are mistaken about one's situation. This is enough to make the greatest coward in the world courageous. Let us be sure to be found within this defended garrison, and sure that we are involved in Zion's concerns; then we shall see all the mountains round about us full of chariots and horses of fire. We shall see Christ reigning, the promise of Christ engaged, and the watchful eye of God upon the church continually. Our fears come from failing to consider these things at all times, and forming carnal views on the basis of things that are seen.

Question 5. *What testimony have we to give to the next generation?*

This testimony consists of two things.

(a) The exercise of faith and patience in all the trials that befall us, so that this may be remembered in the generations to come.

The martyrs that suffered here so long ago still witness to us in this generation, by their faith and patience, that Zion had walls and ramparts round about her, and that God was her God and Guide. Had they not believed this, do you think that they would have given up their bodies to the flames in this city and other parts of the nation? Similarly, that faith and patience which we shall exercise in any trial that shall fall upon us for Zion's sake will tell the generations to come what God has done, and how we have discovered this for ourselves.

(b) It is our duty to pass this on by instructing those who come after us. Our fathers told us what God did in their day, and we are to provide the same testimony of our God. We are to tell our children what God has done in our day: 'For so many years we have professed the faith, we have walked in Zion, and found God faithful in his promise: not one word or tittle has failed of all that the Lord has spoken.' In this way we are to instruct the generation that is growing up, those who have not seen the things that we have seen.

Sermon 9

Christ's Pastoral Care[1]

Shepherd your people with your staff, the flock of your inheritance, who dwell alone in a forest in the midst of a garden land; let them graze in Bashan and Gilead as in the days of old.—Mic. 7:14

I DO not have much to offer to you from these words, yet I cannot give you a proper understanding of the mind of God in them, and of what I wish to say from them, without considering the chapter from the beginning. 'Woe is me! For I have become as when the summer fruit has been gathered, etc.' Some say that when the prophet declares, 'Woe is me,' he is speaking in the name of the earth, viewed as the ground of God's church. I understand him, rather, as speaking in the church's name, the true church of God, found in the midst of a profane but outwardly professing people. The lamentation arises from the prospect of the sin of the people and the misery which was coming upon them. These two things have always been a matter of sorrow for all who truly fear God. They cannot view the sins and the miseries of an outwardly professing people without crying out, 'Woe is me! Sorrow is mine! Sadness of heart belongs

[1] Preached on 16 October, 1673.—G.

to me!' David says, 'My eyes shed streams of tears, because people do not keep your law' (Psa. 119:136). And Jeremiah, when considering the misery and judgments of the people, exclaims, 'Oh that my head were waters, and my eyes a fountain of tears, that I might weep day and night for the slain of the daughter of my people' (Jer. 9:1). The prophet, foreseeing both an overflow of sin and an overflow of judgment, had reason to cry, 'Woe is me! This is my lamentation.'

He gives an account of the state of the professing, visible church, which he compares to a field or vineyard after the harvest is over and the grapes gathered: 'For I have become as when the summer fruit has been gathered, as when the grapes have been gleaned: there is no cluster to eat, no first-ripe fig that my soul desires.' His prayer was that there might be a fruitful vineyard for God, but, 'We are just as when the vintage is over: there are some grapes, some clusters left under the leaves, but the main crop has been removed.' Not only so, but when a field is reaped, or a vineyard gathered, the owner leaves it for a season and removes its fence, so that cattle may enter and roam upon it, until the time for cultivating and composting comes round again. God never leaves a professing church to be a wilderness, not unless it has fallen into utter apostasy. But often he will leave them to be as a field after harvest, or a vineyard after the vintage is gathered. God will leave Babylon as a wilderness that shall never be cultivated again: it shall have no rain, no fences or cultivation. But he will not leave his church in this way, unless there is a final apostasy. However, when a man has gathered his corn from a field you might think he has turned his back on it; the fence is neglected, the animals break in, it is left as if it were common ground.

Men ride over it and trample it down, and the owner leaves it alone. But when the time for cultivation returns, he mends the fence, drives out the cattle, ploughs the field and sows it with good seed, that it may bring forth good fruit. God frequently deals with his church in this way. He breaks the hedges and allows wild beasts to enter, that is, he allows men to ravage the church at will; but there will be a time of cultivating again, when he will ensure a fruit that will be to his praise.

In verse 2 the prophet describes the two elements of the evil of which he is complaining: firstly, that those who were godly were very few; secondly, that those who were evil were very bad. 'The godly has perished from the earth, and there is no one upright among mankind; they all lie in wait for blood, and each hunts the other with a net.' This phrase, 'The godly has perished from the earth,' is not emphasizing so much the fact that godly men are dying, but rather that they have been taken away, and the earth therefore has lost the benefit and advantage that they provided. The same expression is used in Isa. 57:1, 'The righteous man perishes, and no one lays it to heart; devout men are taken away,' and in Psa. 12:1, 'The godly one is gone; for the faithful have vanished from among the children of man.'

Notice from this that when godly men are very few and the bad are very bad, inevitable destruction lies at the door of that place or nation. If either of these is not true then there is still hope. If there had been only ten godly men in Sodom it would have been spared. If the iniquity of the Amorites had not been complete they would not have been ruined. If the good, therefore, are not very few, or the bad not very bad, there is yet hope, but where both occur, as in this case, for this visible church of God, unavoidable destruction is at the door: there is no hope of recovery. Therefore, those who seek to make men godly, to increase the number of the godly, are not only endeavouring to save their own souls but to save the nation from ruin. And this is where we will focus our prayers and concern: we are engaged in this world against the world and against those who reproach us, and our design is to save the nation, as far as we are able. Our design is to increase the number of the godly, to convert men to God, and the result of this will be to preserve the nation. It will be discovered at last that those who are useful in this way do more for the preservation of their country than any army or navy can do. When Micah says, 'The godly has perished from the earth, and there is no one upright among mankind,' it is a hyperbolical expression, indicating that there are only a few who are godly or upright.

The description of the ungodly emphasizes two things: firstly, the nature of their sin, and secondly, the way in which they carried it out. Their sin involved *blood*; the word comprises all violence, oppression, cruelty and persecution. Their prosecution of these evils involved much diligence and effort: 'They all lie in wait for blood, and each hunts the other with a net,' or, as it is expressed in verse 3, 'Their hands are on what is evil, to do it well.' When men lay out all their wisdom, industry and strength in the pursuit of sin, then, particularly, destruction lies at the door. When men are lazy, careless and negligent, sensual in all other things, but diligent in doing evil, here is another situation which the prophet notes as being a certain sign of approaching destruction.

Having described the body of the people in this way, he proceeds to divide them into two groups: the rulers, and the residue of the people. The rulers he divides up into three further sorts: the *prince*, the *judge* and the *great man*. 'The prince and the judge ask for a bribe, and the great man utters the evil desire of his soul' (verse 3). I will not expound these words particularly, but what the prophet is telling us is that when there is a conspiracy, as it were, in all sorts of rulers to commit the same iniquity, and to '*weave*' the business together by agreement amongst themselves – so that there is no one to intercede, no one to stand in the gap, or to behave differently – then the situation is bringing on those judgments which he is about to describe. And this was exactly the state of affairs at this time, for this prophesy dates from the days of Ahaz and there was great agreement and conspiracy among all in power, at that time, to oppress and to pursue their covetous and 'evil desires.' They agreed amongst themselves and 'weaved it together.'

In verse 4, Micah speaks of the remainder of the people. 'The best of them,' he says, 'is like a brier, the most upright of them a thorn hedge.' After having condemned this group generally, he seems to reflect upon some who had pretended to be very friendly towards the church, claiming that they would be a hedge and a fence for it. But, he says, they prove to be briers and a thorn hedge. 'This hypocritical part of the nation, who speak so fairly, and have an appearance of such friendship, yet, when a man places his trust on them, they tear and rend him and give him nothing but trouble and vexation. Whatever pretences they make, there is nothing to be expected from them but what you would expect from thorns and briers.' And I notice that the prophet, when dealing with this hypocritical group, suggests that there will be greater judgment upon them than upon those whose open wickedness he described earlier. For, 'the day of your watchmen, of your punishment has come,' that is, the day which the watchmen had so often declared would come upon them: 'Now their confusion is at hand.' When false professors make an empty pretence of believing the church but in reality intend only further trouble and discomfort – the day of the watchmen is then at hand.

In the fifth and sixth verses he shows that this universal corruption of the people had extended itself to all sorts of relationships – no trust remained, not even among families. 'Put no trust in a neighbour; have no confidence in a friend; guard the doors of your mouth from her who lies in your arms; for the son treats the father with contempt, the daughter rises up against her mother, the daughter-in-law against her mother-in-law; a man's enemies are the men of his own house' (Micah 7:5, 6). It is a sign of extreme turmoil when relationships within families are in disorder and all grounds of confidence between them have decayed. This last verse was particularly applied by our Saviour to the period of the persecution of the gospel (Luke 12:53; Matt. 10:35, 36). No wickedness so corrupts the nature of man and breaks off all confidence in the nearest and strongest relations than enmity towards godliness and persecution of it. 'When they once begin to act in this way,' says the Saviour, 'these will be the consequences.'

With the people of the land being in this state and condition, the prophet, in the name of the church, applies himself in three ways: *firstly*, to God (verse 7); *secondly*, to the church's enemies (verses 8, 10); *thirdly*, to himself (verse 9).

Firstly: With this knowledge of their state and condition, he applies to God: 'But as for me, I will look to the Lord; I will wait for the God of my salvation; my God will hear me' (verse 7). When all things are confused and at a loss, the people of God are not discouraged from looking to God; they are encouraged to do so; indeed, it is quite necessary for them to do so. Not to be looking specifically to God at such a time would be evidence of a heart that was indifferent to the state of God's church.

Secondly: The prophet, on behalf of the church, confronts her enemies. 'Rejoice not over me, O my enemy; when I fall, I shall rise; when I sit in darkness, the Lord will be a light to me … Then my enemy will see, and shame will cover her who said to me, "Where is the Lord your God?" My eyes will look upon her; now she will be trampled down like the mire of the streets' (verses 8, 10).

We may note here:

1. Who this enemy is: 'My enemy.' Some refer this to one thing, others to another. It certainly refers to some false church: perhaps Babylon, or Samaria, or the false professors among themselves. I take it to refer, most probably, to the false worshippers of Dan and Bethel, the false church that dwelt in the same land as themselves. There is no greater enemy to the true church of God than the false church.

2. The way in which the enemy manifested their enmity. The prophet doesn't speak of those outward enemies who attacked and destroyed them, but of those who said to the church, 'Where is the Lord your God?'; the enemy who

reproached them with their profession of faith in God, their nearness to God, and God's acceptance of them. This is continually the reproach of the false church. Those who are open heathens are not so concerned with this, but the usual taunt of the false church is, 'Where is the Lord your God? Where are your prayers and trust in God? Where is your confidence in him?'

3. The church suggests that there were some circumstances in her present state, in God's providence, which the enemy had taken advantage of in order to reproach her: 'Rejoice not over me, O my enemy, when I fall.' Some failure had given weight to the enemy's taunts. But to all such taunts she replies with her trust in God, 'My God will save me.' She comforts herself that the time was coming when God would certainly destroy the enemy of his church: this enemy, this church of false worshippers, who taunt the true church of God, in their troubles and difficulties, for trusting and confiding in him.

Thirdly: He applies to himself, as representing the church: 'I will bear the indignation of the Lord because I have sinned against him, until he pleads my cause and executes judgment for me' (verse 9). This is a very appropriate response to the present state of affliction: a deep humiliation for sin and a quiet submission to the corrections of God's hands. At the same time, there is expressed the firm resolution of faith to wait until God pleads her cause and executes judgment on her enemies. There seems to be the utmost confidence in this case, 'He will bring me out to the light; I shall look upon his vindication.'

The theme of the whole of this prophecy is the deliverance of the church, and that restoration which was fulfilled in part in the delivery of this people out of captivity many years later. 'A day for the building of your walls! In that day the boundary shall be far extended. In that day they will come to you, from Assyria, etc.' (verses 11, 12). All the people who have been scattered will be gathered to Jerusalem, to worship God in his temple. But having said this, he, as it were, corrects himself, 'But wait; that has not yet happened.' 'But the earth will be desolate because of its inhabitants, for the fruit of their deeds' (verse 13). As if he had said, 'Notwithstanding all this, though God has thoughts and a purpose of mercy for his own hidden, secret people, yet there is a time when he will bring forward the judgments that are due for the provocations of the majority of professors. God will do all these things for his church at the appointed time, but, for all that, 'the earth will be desolate'; there is no avoiding this. The behaviour described in verses 1-4 requires the desolation of the land, because of the wickedness of its inhabitants and as the fruit of their actions.

I have made these brief observations on this part of the chapter in order to describe the situation presented. The land was full of sin and of horrible provocations of God from all sorts of people, from the highest to the lowest. The people of God privately lamented this behaviour, and bore it as their own burden, and trembled at the thoughts of the judgments approaching. God had irrevocably decreed desolation upon the whole land. He had declared that whatever might be his mercy and goodness and his thoughts towards his people, yet the land was to be desolated.

In this state and condition, the prophet makes this request: 'Shepherd your people with your staff, the flock of your inheritance, who dwell alone in a forest in the midst of a garden land; let them graze in Bashan and Gilead as in the days of old' (Mic. 7:14).

What we are told in these words is this:

Observation: *In the most calamitous time, in the greatest flood of sin and judgment, however unavoidable the public judgments, there is still a basis for faith to plead with God for the preservation, safety and deliverance of his people.*

All these things are here decreed: a calamitous period; a flood of sin and judgment; an irreversible purpose of God to destroy the land, Yet, faith, I say, has a basis, even in such a state, to plead with God for the preservation and protection of his secret people. You may say, 'This is not a great matter. It may be that we have heard arguments that God will preserve and deliver them, and even heard of calculations of the time when God will do so, and could say "Amen" to it. Yet, there is no purpose in teaching anything further from these words, other than to encourage faith and belief.' I acknowledge that I cannot go further than this, namely, that I teach that for which I have a warrant to teach, out of duty, and to leave all the rest to God's sovereignty. But if God should decree inevitably to destroy this nation, yet still we have grounds for faith to plead with him for the preservation and deliverance of his own inheritance.

I need go no further than this text to prove this, for the expounding of the text, and the proving of the doctrine, are one and the same thing.

In these words we have:

I. What is prayed for, that for which the prophet pleads, namely, 'Shepherd your people with your staff.'

II. The arguments of faith pleaded by the prophet, even when God had inevitably decreed desolation upon the whole land. There are four of these: (a) that they were God's people, 'Shepherd your people'; (b) that they were the flock of his inheritance, 'Shepherd your people, the flock of your inheritance'; (c) that they 'dwelt alone in a forest in the midst of a garden land'; (d) that God had, in former days, 'let them graze in Bashan and Gilead.'

I shall speak briefly on these points and show you both what is being prayed for, and what arguments faith possesses to present to God. For though God may say with respect to some particular nation, 'Do not continue to pray for it,' he has never said so with respect to his own people.

I. Consider *what the prophet is praying for here*, namely, that God would feed his people with his staff: 'Shepherd your people with your staff.' God is compared here to a shepherd, a comparison which he makes use of very often in the Scriptures. You know how many references I could turn to if I wished to prove the point. God is a shepherd, and Christ is a shepherd, and therefore he says, 'Shepherd your people with your staff.' The Hebrew word used sometimes refers to a *sceptre* by which kings rule; sometimes to a staff; sometimes to a *rod*. It was the implement, whatever it was, that shepherds used in those days. It is mentioned in that great description of God as a shepherd, 'Your rod and your staff,' the second word being the same as that used here. God, as a shepherd, rules his people with a staff, an implement which shepherds use both for guidance and correction. He will not strike his sheep with great, violent instruments, to break their bones and destroy them, but he lets them know that he has a staff in his hand. I understand the text as saying that the staff was principally used for directing the flock, and the prophet's prayer is that God would 'shepherd them with his staff.' We need to dwell on the lesson of this word because I believe it provides a rule of faith for us as to what we should pray, for God's people, in a time such as we have described. The great thing that we should pray for presently is that God would shepherd them, not that God would make them kings, rulers and great men, and give them the necks of their enemies to tread upon, or anything of that nature. 'In such circumstances,' he says, 'your prayer should be that God would shepherd.' There are three things involved in this shepherding of God's flock.

(1) That God would supply their spiritual and temporal needs so that they may be spared from great distress. We find this in Revelation 12:6, 'The woman fled into the wilderness, where she has a place prepared by God, in which she is to be nourished.' While the woman was in the wilderness she was protected by spiritual and temporal supplies that kept her from destruction and distress. This is something, therefore, for which we have a rule of faith that we might pray for when we fear that an inevitable destruction is coming upon a nation. God allows us to pray, and gives us a ground of faith to pray, that for his own people he will provide spiritual and temporal supplies so that they might be kept from great distress.

(2) Involved in this shepherding of the Shepherd is the promise that God will give them pledges, remarkable

pledges, of his tenderness and love, at this distressing time. The same thing is said of Christ, in a similar passage: 'He will tend his flock like a shepherd.' How will he do that? 'He will gather the lambs in his arms; he will carry them in his bosom, and gently lead those that are with young' (Isa. 40:11). Here is a rule of faith for us today: that God will deal with all believers, of all kinds, according to their weakness and wants; that when the day of visitation and the day of perplexity come upon the world, Christ, in his shepherding of us, will suit himself to every condition. Some will be more able to be driven forward, others he must carry in his arms. We must pray, therefore, that he will deal with everyone according to their state and condition.

(3) The shepherding involves ruling, protecting and delivering; present rule, and protection and deliverance in God's appointed time. A shepherd not only has to carry his flock into good pasture but has to protect them also from any evil to which they are exposed. David, that great shepherd, who was a type of Christ, gave this account of his work: 'Your servant used to keep sheep for his father. And when there came a lion, or a bear, and took a lamb from the flock, I went after him and struck him and delivered it out of his mouth. And if he arose against me, I caught him by his beard and struck him and killed him' (1 Sam. 17:34, 35). This was part of David's care of the sheep, as their shepherd. The word 'shepherding' used here involves ruling. In chapter 5:4, the same word very clearly means ruling and protecting: 'He shall stand and shepherd his flock,' that is, 'rule' his flock, 'in the strength of the Lord, in the majesty of the name of the Lord his God, and they shall dwell secure.' It is by such shepherding of Christ, in the majesty and power of God,

that his people shall be preserved. In this rule for us, therefore, we are specifically encouraged to pray to this extent: for necessary supplies of spiritual and temporal, inward and outward mercies; grace and mercy towards all, according to the needs of their state and condition; powerful deliverance, in God's good time, for the weak and diseased, and those bearing children.

This is the first thing for which we have a warrant to pray, even at a most disastrous time when inevitable destruction has been decreed against a place or nation.

II. Let us now consider *the arguments that faith has to plead in this situation,* which are found in the text. As I have said, there are four of these. Notice, first, the general point that not one of the arguments is based on any worth or desert, any good or grace, that belongs to the people themselves. They are all taken from God himself, from the relationship he bears to his people and from what he had previously done for them. Whatever we may plead or argue before God, in such a day, for safety and protection, if these arguments are secretly influenced by thoughts that we are good and better than others, there is no faith in them. God knows, all the graces and fruits of all believers and professors in this land, considered in and of themselves, will never make up one argument.

(1) The first argument that the prophet uses is that *they were the people of God*: 'Shepherd your people.' They were his people for three reasons; each of which forms an argument.

(a) *They were a people of God on account of election.* Christ commanded the apostle to continue preaching at Corinth by this argument: 'I am with you, and no one will attack you to harm you, for I have many in this city who are my people' (Acts 18:10). They were the people of God by election. God had eternally chosen them and purposed that they should be converted by the gospel, by the preaching of Paul's ministry.

Does this supply an argument to plead with God? Yes: 'Will not God give justice to his elect, who cry to him day and night? Will he delay long over them? I tell you, he will give justice to them speedily' (Luke 18:7, 8). The argument for justice arises from the fact that the people are his elect: 'Will he not give justice to his elect?' There is something in the decree of God's election and choice of his people which may be pleaded before him for the pre-eminent work of shepherding, namely, the avenging of them over their enemies.

(b) They are the people of God *by purchase and possession*. This was the great plea under the Old Testament: The people of the Lord, whom he has redeemed 'with a strong hand and an outstretched arm' (Psa. 136:12), whom he has taken out of the world and planted for himself. Micah made it an argument to plead with God, that they were his people by purchase and possession. The argument has grown so much stronger under the gospel, in that they are purchased by the blood of his Son: 'He who did not spare his own Son but gave him up for us all, how will he not also with him graciously give us all things?' (Rom. 8:32). The people we plead for are God's elect people and he will give justice to them speedily; they are God's purchased people, even purchased by the blood of his Son. And will he not also with him give them all things, all necessary things, all things that pertain to life and godliness? Here is a basis for faith to plead with God in such a case.

(c) They are God's people *by covenant*. The relationship between God and his people is prepared beforehand by election, purchase, possession and redemption, but the formal appointment of it arises from the covenant: 'They shall be my people, and I will be their God ... I will make with them an everlasting covenant' (Jer. 32:38-40). This finalises the relationship. Hosea 2:23 conveys the same truth.

What are the arguments derived from the fact that they are God's covenant people? The summation of everything that may be pleaded on that basis, and they are great and numerous, is declared in Luke 1:68-75, 'Blessed be the Lord God of Israel, for he has visited and redeemed his people and has raised up a horn of salvation for us ... as he spoke by the mouth of his holy prophets from of old, that we should be saved from our enemies and from the hand of all who hate us; to show the mercy promised to our fathers and to remember his holy covenant, the oath that he swore to our father Abraham, to grant us that we, being delivered from the hand of our enemies, might serve him without fear, in holiness and righteousness before him all our days.' We have a right to pray for everything here: everything that is included in God's shepherding of us. And what is the argument on which it is based? God will 'remember his holy covenant, the oath that he swore.' By this oath it is established. Therefore, he will establish us that we 'might serve him without fear, in holiness and righteousness before him all our days.' What a great argument we have for those for whom we pray: that they are God's covenant people! 'Lord, "shepherd your people," those who are yours by election, by purchase and possession, and those who are yours by covenant: a people who have made a covenant with you.'

(2) The second argument is: Because *they are 'the flock of your inheritance.'* There are two things here that we might argue in prayer with God: (a) That they are a flock; (b) That they are 'the flock of God's inheritance.'

(a) They are 'a flock'; that is, of sheep. And so these three further things may be pleaded before God: (i) They are helpless; (ii) harmless; (iii) useful.

(i) A flock of sheep is *helpless.* Sheep are weak, helpless creatures; the more of them there are in the flock, the more exposed they are to every kind of plundering and destruction. And truly, God's people are the same, unless Christ, their shepherd, is with them. They are, and have been, a weak, helpless people throughout the world. I acknowledge that when Christ, their shepherd, is with them, they triumph over great difficulties, but of themselves they are completely helpless.

(ii) They are *harmless.* No harm comes from sheep, and all the saints of God are commanded to be similar: 'Be blameless and innocent ('harmless,' KJV), in the midst of a crooked and twisted generation' (Phil. 2:15). Let us not harm the world, in public or in private – do them no wrong or injury – so that we might have an argument from this to plead with God.

(iii) Sheep are *useful.* I will mention three things where God's people are useful to the world (though I do not usually enjoy using much allegorical detail). Firstly, by the secret blessing that accompanies them; secondly, by the good example they provide; thirdly, by their industry in the world.

Firstly, there is *a secret blessing* that accompanies God's people. This may be seen in the prophecy of Micah 5:7, 'The remnant of Jacob shall be in the midst of many peoples like dew from the Lord, like showers on the grass, which delay not for a man nor wait for the children of man.' This poor remnant of Jacob, dwelling among the people, communicates a secret blessing to them; a blessing that puts a spring in their step, like the dew. They receive this because of the remnant of Jacob in their midst. Do people see it? No, it is not a visible thing; it 'delays not for a man.' No one sees the secret way by which the dew falls, or those secret ways by which blessings are communicated to the whole nation from the presence of the remnant of Jacob amongst them.

Secondly, they are useful because of *their good example*: walking in this world in a way that is becoming for creatures made for the glory of God. 'The saying is trustworthy, and I want you to insist on these things, so that those who have believed in God may be careful to devote themselves to good works. These things are excellent and profitable to people' (Titus 3:8). It is not only those who are helped who profit from these good works, but all of mankind. When believers are diligent and fruitful in good works, all mankind is profited by their example.

Thirdly, they are profitable and *useful* to the world by their industry in it. 'Let our people learn to devote themselves to good works ('profess honest trades'; KJV, margin), so as to help cases of urgent need, and not be unfruitful' (Titus 3:14). Many others only consume the fruits of the earth in luxury and waste, but God enables these to work hard at their 'honest trades.' There is an argument for prayer here: that this flock is helpless, harmless, fruitful and useful.

(b) But the strongest argument lies in the second phrase, 'Shepherd the flock of your inheritance.' This flock is God's *heritage*; 'The Lord's portion is his people, Jacob his allotted heritage' (Deut. 32:9). Why are they described as his 'allotted' heritage? When the people came to possess the land, it was divided up by lot. God has his allotted portion in the world. That which has fallen to God's share, if I may put it in that way, is this flock; and Christ rejoices in it. 'You hold my lot. The lines have fallen for me in pleasant places; indeed, I have a beautiful inheritance' (Psa. 16:5, 6). His lot was cast in Canaan: a good and fruitful place. Christ views his church and is satisfied with it. 'I desire nothing more,' he says. 'The lines have fallen for me in pleasant places. This, my lot, is a beautiful inheritance.'

The following things may be pleaded in prayer from this truth that they are 'the flock of God's inheritance':

(i) As they are God's inheritance, if God does not take care of it, nobody else will. Every man takes care of his own inheritance, that which belongs to him. If God does not take care of his, there is nobody else to care for them. It is often said that they are those for whom no one cares. Why is this? Because no one owns them as an inheritance. They are not the heritage of princes or of the great men of the world; not of the Turk or the Pope. They are God's inheritance; if he does not care for them, it is vain to expect care from any other source.

(ii) It is the inheritance of him whom the world considers its greatest enemy. The whole world is at enmity against God, and you see the state of the world. Everyone is determined to destroy his inheritance. Look at all the nations abroad, in all their tumults: their main design is to ruin this heritage, because it is God's. Against him they maintain this enmity in their hearts, worship and ways. If therefore God does not maintain his inheritance it will certainly be destroyed, for the very reason that it is his.

(iii) The following argument may also be pleaded: If this flock is God's inheritance, then, if it is taken away, the whole is hell. If God's lot is gone, if this remnant is destroyed, then, however much men may try to make everything as fine as they can, decorate their dungeon as much as they please, it is all only hell.

These are the arguments that may be pleaded in prayer with God from the facts that the flock is weak, helpless and harmless, and yet useful to the glory of God and the good of men. It is God's inheritance: if he does not care for it, no one will, and if it is removed from the earth, that earth will soon become a hell.

(3) The third argument is taken from their state and condition: 'They dwell alone in a forest in the midst of a garden land.' The first argument pleaded God's glory, love and faithfulness: 'thy flock.' The second pleaded God's interest:

'the flock of your inheritance.' This third argument pleads God's pity and compassion: 'who dwell alone in a forest in the midst of a garden land.' In this case, every word carries an argument that may be pleaded with God.

(a) 'They dwell alone'; that is, dejectedly. It is a weak, dejected flock, living far from any help. Two things are referred to here: inward dejection, due to their own fears and distresses, and outward helplessness. Their situation is such that no one visits them to relieve them. This provides a strong plea: the solitariness of God's flock, and the compassion and mercy of God for their relief. It may be that because of our peace and plenty, and the things that we enjoy, we are not as aware of the strength of this argument. But the Lord knows, and many of his people understand, how strong a plea it is with God in reality: 'We are a weak, solitary people; comfortless within and helpless without.'

(b) They dwell alone, and 'they dwell in a forest'; that is, in a dark and entangled condition. They are not only dejected, alone and helpless, but also in the dark, so that they do not see their way and are in danger of wandering. If they do stray from the path, the animals of the wood are ready to devour them. There is nothing more difficult for God's people these days than the fact that that they are in a forest where it is hard to see one's way. The Lord makes them careful and helps them to see the Saviour's footsteps going before them, so that they are kept from wandering and from the danger of the wild beasts.

(c) Another plea arises from the situation of the forest; it is in the midst of a garden land (Hebrew: 'of Carmel').

Though there was a particular place called 'Carmel,' the word is a common name for a fruitful field for feeding. The country or land in which they lived was such a field. Some think that this refers to Babylon, which was very fruitful for its inhabitants, but this poor remnant dwells in a forest in the middle of a garden land. This was true of the Jews. Nehemiah provides a most pathetic description of their state, 'Behold, we are slaves this day; in the land that you gave to our fathers to enjoy its fruits and its good gifts, behold, we are slaves. And its rich yield goes to the kings whom you have set over us because of our sins. They rule over our bodies and over our livestock as they please, and we are in great distress' (Neh. 9:36, 37). These people lived 'in a forest in the midst of a garden land,' yet they were in a distressed condition.

(d) And there is yet another plea in these words: a plea for mercy. They are not only solitary for some brief period in the forest, but they *dwell* there. They have been there a long time, and may continue there for a long time further. It symbolizes an abiding, continuing state. This argument has regard to the pity, the mercies of God, his compassion and tenderness, when his poor people continue for a long time in an embarrassed, perplexed state, as if in a wood in the midst of a garden land, given by God to their fathers. It is a picture of many of God's people today, and it is a great plea for mercy and compassion.

(4) There is one last argument in these words, which I shall only mention and then conclude. Let them 'graze in Bashan and Gilead as in the days of old.' Bashan and Gilead were two very fruitful places. This is why the children of Reuben

and Gad asked Moses that they might have their possession in Gilead and in the kingdom of Bashan: '[Because it] is a land for livestock, and your servants have livestock' (Num. 32:4). It was a fertile land where their flocks were well fed and nourished.

Where is the argument here? It derives from a former experience of God's actions: from a knowledge of his faithfulness, based on past experience. 'We have seen what God can do, how he brought his people out of distresses, carried them through difficulties, delivered them out of troubles, and fed them in Bashan and in the land of Gilead.' This knowledge was the basis of their plea that he would feed them in the same way again.

I could take this argument further, but will leave it now. I think that what I have discussed is not untimely. We have seen what is presented to us, namely, that we have a rule of faith for what to pray for in times like the present: that God would 'shepherd his flock.' We have seen what this involves and have briefly considered the arguments that may be brought before God in such a case, leaving the times and seasons to his own sovereignty.

———

PURITAN 🕴 PAPERBACKS

PURITAN 🎩 PAPERBACKS

PURITAN ![logo] PAPERBACKS

BANNER
of **TRUTH**

The Banner of Truth Trust originated in 1957 in London. The founders believed that much of the best literature of historic Christianity had been allowed to fall into oblivion and that, under God, its recovery could well lead not only to a strengthening of the church, but to true revival.

Inter-denominational in vision, this publishing work is now international, and our lists include a number of contemporary authors along with classics from the past. The translation of these books into many languages is encouraged.

A monthly magazine, *The Banner of Truth*, is also published. More information about this and all our publications can be found on our website or supplied by either of the offices below.

Head Office:
3 Murrayfield Road
Edinburgh
EH12 6EL
United Kingdom
Email: info@banneroftruth.co.uk

North America Office:
610 Alexander Spring Road
Carlisle, PA 17015
United States of America
Email: info@banneroftruth.org